I T A L Y

GOOD STORIES REVEAL as much, or more, about a locale as any map or guidebook. Whereabouts Press is dedicated to publishing books that will enlighten a traveler to the soul of a place. By bringing a country's stories to the English-speaking reader, we hope to convey its culture through literature. Books from Whereabouts Press are essential companions for the curious traveler, and for the person who appreciates how fine writing enhances one's experiences in the world.

"Coming newly into Spanish, I lacked two essentials— a childhood in the language, which I could never acquire, and a sense of its literature, which I could."

—Alastair Reid, *Whereabouts: Notes on Being a Foreigner*

ITALY

A TRAVELER'S LITERARY COMPANION

EDITED AND TRANSLATED BY

LAWRENCE VENUTI

WHEREABOUTS PRESS
BERKELEY, CALIFORNIA

Published in the United States by
Whereabouts Press
Berkeley, California
www.whereaboutspress.com

Map of Italy by BookMatters

Manufactured in the United States of America

Library of Congress Cataloging-in-Publication Data

Italy: a traveler's literary companion /
edited and translated by Lawrence Venuti.
p.   cm. — (Traveler's literary companions)
Includes bibliographical references.
1. Short stories, Italian—Translations into English.
2. Italian fiction—20th century—Translations into English.
3. Italy—Fiction.   I. Venuti, Lawrence.
II. Traveler's literary companion.
PQ4257 .E5186   2003
853' .01083245—dc11   2003014080

For Gemma and Jules

Soltanto questo crescere
indifferente allo sguardo e pieno
di ciò che ha visto
era possibile: se ci sono
due barche
non contava il loro punto d'incontro, ma la bellezza
del cammino dentro l'acqua . . .

Only this growing
indifferent to the glance and full
of what was seen
was possible: if there are
two boats
it isn't their meeting point that mattered, but the beauty
of the journey in the water . . .

SOUTHERN ITALY

Contents

In effect, the selections offer a panorama of modern Italian fiction, even if restricted by space limitations, and the reader is invited to sketch a time line through the dates of publication printed after the pieces. Many of them address the various changes that have shaped Italy during the twentieth century, presenting a historical perspective that is not only literary but social. The impact of the Fascist regime in the 1920s and 1930s, the economic boom in the late 1950s, the feminist movement in the 1960s, and the influx of eastern European immigrants in the 1990s can all be glimpsed against the backdrop of broader, national trends like the uneven distribution of wealth and industry that has driven so many southern Italians to emigrate to the north.

The most crucial criterion for selection, however, was geography. I searched for stories set in specific Italian locales, in most cases stories that don't just mention place names, but somehow make the place a significant element in the narrative. Major stops on the tourist route are covered: Rome, Florence, Venice, Naples, Capri. These pieces unfold around famous landmarks and monuments and even mention particular streets, thus giving the traveler a layer of resonance beyond the information dispensed in a guidebook. The plan to provide a native view of Italy also led me to include stories set in cities and regions that travelers might not ordinarily visit but that nonetheless loom large in the Italian imagination: Turin, Milan, the Veneto, Trieste, Palermo. Because modern Italian writers do not consistently specify settings, preferring to endow their work with a more abstract or universal significance, the emphasis on place results in an unusual view of the litera-

ture for readers of translations, a view that foregrounds
lesser-known writers and uncommon themes.

For one thing, this emphasis highlights regional varia-
tions in Italian society. The stories depict members of every
social rank, although the representations tend to differ with
location. Bourgeois complacency is ridiculed by both Luigi
Malerba and Goffredo Parise, but it takes divergent forms
in Rome and in the industrial north. Humorous treatments
likewise vary according to place and class, as with the
socialites in Aldo Palazzeschi's urban satire or the vendor
of religious images in Barbara Alberti's ribald vignettes of
rural life. Even a quietly moving piece is decisively inflected
by geography. Mario Rigoni Stern's modest fable of a
lovelorn sawmill worker gradually acquires a mythological
dimension that befits the wooded areas of the Veneto.

The stories also address a wide spectrum of occupations
that might be of special interest to travelers simply because
a trip to Italy can involve some exposure to them. The cast
of characters includes a waiter and a train conductor, a
concierge at a pensione and the owner of a bar, a tailor and
a dressmaker, a foreign consul and a police inspector. These
characters are not always portrayed as tourists see them,
busy on the job, but as Italians might meet them, neighbors going about their daily lives.

The results are often surprising, sometimes disturbing.
Magris's Jewish musician recalls how his father admired
Mussolini before the Fascists instituted the racial laws in
1938. In Ginzburg's anguished tale, a single mother con-
fronts a death wish only to be finally reunited with her children. Malerba's insouciant father is relieved to learn that
his bored teenaged son has taken an interest in a motor-

cycle, even though that interest turns out to be criminal. Such stories cast doubt on any conventional notion of the happy, gregarious Italian family by showing how various circumstances—personal, social, political—profoundly unsettle the characters' lives.

The geographical approach unearthed several stories that might be particularly revealing to the traveler because they examine relations between Italians and foreign tourists. Pirandello uses a Sicilian narrator to scrutinize the cliché that the British are emotionally repressed. Domenico Rea demonstrates how Italians sometimes stereotype Americans: his Neapolitan narrator has constructed an unflattering image of American women that is abruptly redefined by a chance encounter. The now widespread view that Hollywood is a force of cultural imperialism abroad already underlies Massimo Bontempelli's 1925 fantasy about an Italian film actor who unexpectedly suffers from his work for an American director. Antonio Tabucchi puts both American and French tourists to strategic use as the unassuming bystanders in his Florentine Gothic.

Italian writers have similarly been concerned with the experiences that their countrymen undergo as travelers in their native country. This theme is explored in diverse ways, depending on whether the trip functions as business or pleasure. Maraini follows a woman whose work as a lawyer requires her, not only to commute between Milan and Rome, but to shift between two very different lives. Parise satirizes the nouveaux riches who vacation at Portofino, whereas Corrado Alvaro evokes the painful Neapolitan honeymoon taken by a newlywed couple from a village in Campania. Regional prejudices are sometimes apparent. Romano Bilenchi probes the psychology of a young boy who must endure a Florentine bias against the coastal area of Tuscany. And Capri will never look the same—regardless of the reader's nationality—after the campy surrealism of Alberto Savinio's travelogue, where the ghost of the emperor Tiberius hovers mysteriously in the background.

Taken together, the stories point up cultural differences that challenge familiar images of Italy. The translations also pursue this defamiliarizing aim, but at the level of the sentence. I have employed strategies that not only imitate the distinctive styles and tones of the individual pieces, but also seek to signal their cultural origins by retaining Italian words and phrases. Some of the Italian is quite common, likely to be heard every day by tourists; other uses of the language will seem strange at first. In context, however, all of it quickly becomes intelligible and at points subtly suggestive, taking on meanings that go beyond the Italian text. When, for example, Rea's narrator describes his companion's laughter as "all'americana," it clearly means "in the manner of an American woman," but in the English version it hardens into a pejorative stereotype. The translations are designed to give the reader another opportunity to travel: in their deviations from current English usage, they open up the reading experience to the foreignness of a different language for translation, although in a way that is enjoyably engaging. Such, at least, is my hopeful intention.

~

This book would not have been possible without David Peattie's inspiring confidence in my abilities as an editor and translator. John Shepley's fluent version of Alberto Savinio's travel piece acted as a different sort of inspiration by moving me to cultivate a style that deviated from his English choices while adhering more closely to the Italian author's tone. Marina Guglielmi helped me to establish an insider's perspective by recommending a number of writers and texts when the project was just getting off the ground. Miriam Fried read most of the stories on the eve of her first Italian journey and responded with encouraging enthusiasm. Kate Warne copyedited the finished versions with care and sensitivity.

Martha Tennent carefully examined every translation, making incisive criticisms and suggesting alternative phrasings. As a native speaker of English who has long lived abroad, she has an unusual take on the language which enabled me to discover some felicitous renderings that would have otherwise remained beyond my grasp. Of course, she can't be held responsible for the final versions (even if she is a most *simpatica* travel companion).

The lines in the dedication are drawn from Milo De Angelis's poem, "Soltanto," which appeared in his collection *Somiglianze* (Milan: Guanda, 1976). The English version was published in my translation of his work, *Finite Intuition: Selected Poetry and Prose* (Los Angeles: Sun & Moon, 1995).

I dedicate this book to my children, with whom I lived one fateful year in Italy—and hope to do so once again.

Lawrence Venuti
NEW YORK CITY, JUNE 2003

ITALY

Summer
Natalia Ginzburg

I STAYED AWAY from my children for a while. They were at the sea with my sister and mother, I remained in the city, in Turin. My mother was angry with me because I didn't stay in touch and seldom wrote. I mentioned work commitments, which really didn't exist. I was living in a pensione where the concierge stank, her body and clothing gave off an odor that on hot days grew more intense, more violent. Every morning I went to the office but worked little; more than anything else I went to the office to pretend I was a man, I was weary of being a woman. For a while everybody enjoys assuming a role that isn't hers, and I played at being a man, I sat behind a huge filthy desk at the office and ate in an osteria, I dawdled in the streets and in cafés with

---

Born in Palermo, NATALIA GINZBURG *(1916–1991) grew up in Turin. She married an anti-Fascist intellectual who died soon after he was imprisoned under Mussolini's dictatorship. Ginzburg published autobiographical novels, stories, and essays—some dark, others humorous, all compelling in their affecting lyricism. Much of her work has been translated into English, including* The Road to the City *(1942) and* Family Sayings *(1963).*

friends, men and women, I went home late at night. It amazed me that my life had once been different, when I had dandled my babies and cooked and cleaned, I thought about how there are so many ways to live, and everybody can turn themselves into a new person at any time, even into an enemy of a former self. But then the part I played also wound up boring me, I kept on leading the same sort of life without getting the slightest pleasure. Still, I didn't want to go to my mother's by the sea, I wanted to stay away from my children, to be alone; I sensed I couldn't be with my children the way I was now, with that deep feeling of disgust, I sensed I would've felt disgust for them too if I'd seen them. So many times I thought I was like the elephants who hide when they're about to die. They hide to die—in the jungle they search at length for a sheltered spot dense with trees, so as to hide the shame of their huge weary dying bodies. It was summer, the summer was hot, scorching the huge city, and when I bicycled down the asphalt viale beneath the trees, my heart shrank with feelings of both repulsion and love for every street, for every house in that city, and they hid various kinds of memories, burning like the sun, as I fled ringing my bell. Giovanna was waiting for me in a café one evening when I left the office, and I sat next to her at the table, showed her the letters from my mother. She knew I wanted to die, and because of this we didn't have much to say, we just sat next to each other, smoking, blowing out the smoke through closed lips. I wanted to die because of a man, but then because of so many other things as well, because I owed my mother some money, and because the concierge at the pensione stank, and because the summer was hot, scorching, in a city filled with mem-

ories and streets, and because I thought I couldn't be of use
to anybody the way I was.

Just as one day my children had lost their father, they
would also lose their mother, but it didn't matter much,
because disgust and shame assail us at a certain moment in
our lives, and no one has the power to help us then. It was a
Sunday afternoon, I'd bought some sleeping pills in a pharmacy. I walked through the empty city all day, thinking
about myself and my children. I was gradually losing the
awareness of their youth, the timbre of their childish voices
faded inside me; I told them everything, about the sleeping
pills and the elephants, about the concierge at the pensione
and what they had to do when they grew up, how they had
to act to protect themselves from what happens. But all of a
sudden I saw them again as I did the last time, sitting on the
ground playing skittles. And the echo of thoughts and words
reverberated through me in the silence, I was amazed to
realize how alone I was, alone and free in the empty city, with
the power to harm myself in any way I wished. I went home
and took the sleeping pills, I shook all the pills from the bottle into a glass of water, I really didn't know if I wanted to
sleep a very long time or die. In the morning the concierge
arrived, she found me asleep and after a little while she went
to call a doctor. I stayed in bed a week, and Giovanna came
every day and brought me oranges and ice. I told her that
anyone who's conceived a heartfelt disgust shouldn't live,
and she smoked in silence and looked at me, blowing out the
smoke through closed lips. Other friends came too, and
everybody told me what they thought, everybody wanted to
teach me what I had to do now. But I said that anyone who's
conceived a heartfelt disgust shouldn't live.

Giovanna told me to leave the pensione and go stay with her. She lived with a Danish girl who walked barefoot through the rooms. At this point I no longer desired to die, but neither did I desire to live, and I dawdled at the office or in the streets, with friends, men and woman, people who wanted to teach me how I had to save myself. In the morning Giovanna slipped on a prune-colored dressing gown, brushed her hair from her forehead and tossed me a disdainful greeting. In the morning the Danish girl entered the room barefoot and started to type up all the dreams she'd had. One night she dreamt that she took an axe and killed her father and mother. And yet she loved her father and mother a great deal. They were waiting for her in Copenhagen but she didn't want to return, because she said we need to live far away from our roots. She read her mother's letters aloud to us. Giovanna's mother was dead, and Giovanna had arrived too late to see her die, when she was alive they'd tried in vain to talk. I said a mother is useful only to her babies, when they're little, to nurse and dandle them, but later she's absolutely useless and there's no point in trying to talk. The simplest things can't even be said, so how can she help? Trying to talk breeds a silence that is actually a burden. I said, I'm absolutely useless to my children because they don't need to be nursed and dandled any more, they're kids with dirty knees and patched pants, and they aren't even big enough for you to try to talk to them. But Giovanna said there's really only one way to live, and that's to board a train for some faraway country, perhaps at night. At home she had everything she needed to take a trip, she had so many thermoses and all kinds of suitcases and even a little bag for vomiting when you go on an airplane. The Danish girl told me I had to write down my dreams, because dreams tell us what we need to do, and she told me I had to reflect upon my childhood and talk about it, because the secret of what we are is hidden in our childhood. But at this point my childhood seemed to me so remote and faraway, and my mother's face was remote, and I was weary of thinking about myself so much, I wanted to look at other people and understand how I was. So I resumed people-watching while I dawdled in the cafés and the streets, men and women with their children, perhaps someone had once experienced that heartfelt disgust, then time had passed and she'd forgotten it. Perhaps someone had once waited in vain on a street corner, or someone had walked in silence through a dusty city for an entire day, or someone had looked into a dead man's face and asked for his forgiveness. One day I received a letter from my mother, who told me the children had scarlet fever. Then the old maternal anxiety paralyzed my heart. I boarded a train and departed. Giovanna came to the station with me, she yearned to sniff the scent of the trains, brushing her hair from her forehead with her disdainful smile.

Leaning my forehead against the window, I watched the city draw away, now devoid of any evil power, cold and innocuous as spent charcoal. The old maternal anxiety that I knew so well wreaked havoc inside me with the roar of the train, a whirlwind sweeping away the Danish girl, Giovanna, the concierge at the pensione, the sleeping pills and the elephants, and I asked myself how I could've spent an entire summer caring about so many useless things.

(1964)

Well Off

Goffredo Parise

ONE DAY MR. AND MRS. TRUPÌA, proprietors of a distillery, embarked with their family for Portofino, where Mr. Trupìa wished to purchase a boat for summer holidays. Mr. Trupìa, a native of southern Italy, felt ashamed of his origins, so he described himself as a native of Trento and had learned a smattering of the Trentine dialect, as well as a smattering of Lombard. He felt ashamed of being Italian too and would have liked to be born, like many of his relatives, in America. For this reason he and his wife jestingly called themselves Mr. and Mrs., but only the wife had acquired a smattering of English; she belonged to the Lombard bourgeoisie and twenty years earlier had spent two months in England to "learn the language." She knew a thing or two, would read the American edition of *Vogue*,

Born in Vicenza, GOFFREDO PARISE *(1929–1986) wrote journalism as well as novels and stories. His nonfiction includes books about China, Vietnam, and Biafra. His fiction tends to combine realism with satire in addressing social issues. Several of his works are available in English, including* The Abecedary *(1972) and* Solitudes *(1982).*

and had enlightened her husband as to the most intimate meanings of Mr. and Mrs.

They embarked in an amaranthine-colored Jaguar MKIO, which was registered in the firm's name. Mr. Trupìa could not afford a Jaguar MKIO (whether or not it was amaranthine-colored), much less a boat, and even less registering both in the firm's name. The firm was essentially a warehouse that possessed the sinister appearance of a crematorium; it sat on the banks of a stream that flowed through the nearby village and emptied into the Po. The number of workers varied between twenty and thirty, what with the constant hiring and firing to avoid paying union wages, and the work lasted eight or nine months each year. Business ran in dribs and drabs: grappa production in Italy was prodigious, nearly all of it poor quality, and sales were stiffly competitive. But Mr. Trupìa maintained that he had "a nose for business" and proceeded according to his "nose," which brought him very often before the magistrate and the tribunal. He told his wife, "The important thing is always to agree with everyone, to take your time, and to do what you want. The lawyers will take care of the rest."

The firm's warehouse, constructed at night and without any permit, collapsed, resulting in one dead and two injured. Facing a prison sentence on that occasion, Mr. Trupìa told the workers (all in white shirts), "They want to put me in prison, I who built this factory with my own hands, who feed so many families, who represent progress in this town of envious freeloaders."

The workers demonstrated on his behalf, and through some unknown means Mr. Trupìa avoided prison. He then bought a house near the distillery from a ninety-year-old dentist. The dentist died, and Mr. Trupìa stopped making payments to the dentist's heirs, while beginning renovations according to his plan for an extension: eight guest rooms and eight bathrooms, a washable nylon carpet, a terrace garden with a barbecue, a swimming pool and a very high wall topped with bottle shards and erected on public land. The mayor ordered that the wall be demolished, but to the mayor's ordinances Mr. Trupìa responded thus, "In response to your Honor's ordinance of the twenty-fourth of last month . . ." Months passed during which Mr. Trupìa affirmed that he had already complied. The wall was finally demolished at municipal expense in the presence of carabinieri, but it slowly started to rise again a few days later.

Mr. Trupìa told his wife, "The important thing in life is to act, to build; the law is the consolation of the petty, of those who can't act. This is why lawyers exist." His way of thinking would not have been shared by his father-in-law, an honest grappa maker who went bankrupt in 1929 and paid every last debt. Thanks to this conduct, he recovered, prospered, and then died, leaving everything to his daughter who needed to get married in a hurry and hence became Mrs. Trupìa.

Mr. Trupìa had a burly brother who was interested almost exclusively in football, but would have liked to be a boxer. He had owned and lost a bar. He also had a wife and three children. He was hired without any particular responsibilities and often served as a figurehead in various property transfers for the firm. Secretly, however, Mr. Trupìa thought of him as his "gorilla." One day Mr. Trupìa drove through a village at a very high speed and was stopped by a policeman who planted himself in the middle of the road. Mr. Trupìa said, "Take my license number; I'm in a hurry." He was about to continue on his way, but the policeman would not permit him. Mr. Turpìa nodded to his brother, who got out of the car and slugged the policeman. At that moment, Mr. Trupìa thought, "The important thing is to act; what counts are deeds. I will continue on my way; Salvatore will go to jail." Salvatore, the "gorilla," served a six-month jail sentence and upon his release continued to play the "gorilla" for Mr. Trupìa.

Mrs. Trupìa loved her husband a great deal and considered him a "new man" compared to her father, whom she had loved during her childhood and adolescence, whose memory she respected, but whom she had always considered an "old man." Her father did not travel, never went on vacation (except to Montecatini for a course of treatments), wore a moustache and a goatee, and did his accounts with a fountain pen to check what the secretary had done with a calculator. He was gentle (he would often get teary-eyed, even at the table), as well as boring and hopelessly "old." With her husband, however, she went to Casino di Campione, Tokyo (an unfruitful attempt to sell grappa to the Japanese), Porto Rotondo (Sardegna), and New York. Not even Americans would buy grappa. Still, one needed only to spread its fame throughout the world with a strong publicity campaign and everything else would fall into place.

Mr. Trupìa also spoke of economy and found that the practice of saving typical of the old bourgeoisie was passé, that the new bourgeoisie, to which he was certain he belonged, was based instead on personal initiative and credit. At the same time, although declaring that he was a socialist, he thought it necessary to defend himself against enemies, and to this end he bought three automatic rifles of the type issued to the American armed forces in Vietnam. Mr. Trupìa naturally underwent many court proceedings, from which he would often absent himself by providing a medical certificate; for this reason, two carabinieri were frequently stationed in front of his house and occasionally entered it to ascertain whether he was in fact ill. Mr. Trupìa would not be at home, nor would he be ill, and for his failure to appear he underwent still other proceedings. The magistrate always waited for a sufficient number of charges to accumulate before issuing a warrant for his arrest; when the number of charges was not sufficient, Mr. Trupìa was ordered to pay fines (which he did not pay), and either the fine fell outside the statute of limitations or he was granted an amnesty.

The manufacture of the grappa, made by mixing the dregs from various kinds of pressed grapes which came mostly from Sicily and Puglia, resulted in waste products that were dumped into the stream next to the distillery. For many years the inhabitants of the village would fish there for eel, tench, trout, and even shrimp. Now the water had turned reddish and turbid, it emitted a terrible odor of putrefaction, and the villagers had to keep their windows closed. There were many petitions, on-the-spot inspections by the public health officer, and ordinances from the mayor. Mr. Trupìa declared that he was willing to install a purification plant, but years passed and this never happened; on the contrary, the workers also received orders to dump plastic bags into the stream. In the presence of carabinieri, the drains of the distillery were sealed, but during the night they exploded.

An animal lover who lived next to the distillery kept many animals in his house and garden, including a talking Indian blackbird who insistently issued commands to a parrot. He would say, "Loreto, say ciao to me. Loreto bello, say ciao to me; say ciao to me, Loreto." And every so often Loreto would respond, "Ciao." During the manufacture of the grappa neither the blackbird nor the parrot would speak. The parrot was by nature restive, but the blackbird was a regular blabbermouth.

Mr. and Mrs. Trupìa's family was composed of three children—two boys and a girl named Gianluigi, Gianluca, and Fabrizia, respectively. An aunt from Calabria who wore very thick glasses lived in the house, in a ground-floor room with barred windows that looked out onto the road. The aunt spent every daylight hour standing before one of the barred windows, looking at the road, and playing with marbles which, with a smile, she would make click a few centimeters from her eyes. Many children watched her with admiration because she was very skillful at the game.

The daughter Fabrizia, who was sixteen years old, would never eat fish. This was not simply a problem for the family, because if Fabrizia saw other people eating fish she would begin to retch. The son Gianluigi, who was eighteen, loved cross-country motorcycle racing and Che Guevara. He had a Che Guevara T-shirt. He considered his father bourgeois and had taken drugs in London, where he spent three days instead of three months, returning because of homesickness. Gianluca was twenty and attended a school for chemists. In a few weeks he would be married to the pregnant daughter of a real estate agent, but his great passion in life was to be a film director, a reporter, or a "high-level" photojournalist. He read only nonfiction and had made two short 16 mm films, one about a mental hospital, the other—entitled *Poppy*—about a pop music festival in Rome. For the moment, however, Gianluca's problem was whether to have a straight or a countercultural wedding and whether to require the guests to wear formal attire or hippie retro. Gianluca's problem was never resolved, nor did the family arrive in Portofino to eat fish (despite Fabrizia's revulsion): they died on the highway in the vicinity of Pavia, after colliding with a tow truck. The myopic aunt, the one with the marbles, survived because they had left her at home for lack of space.

(1997)

The Bewitched Jacket

Dino Buzzati

ALTHOUGH I APPRECIATE elegant dress, I don't usually pay attention to the perfection (or imperfection) with which my companions' clothing is cut.

Nonetheless, one night during a reception at a house in Milan, I met a man about forty years old who literally shone because of the simple and decisive beauty of his clothes.

I don't know who he was, I was meeting him for the first time, and at our introduction, as always happens, it was impossible to get his name. But at a certain point during the evening, I found myself near him, and we began to talk. He seemed a civil, well-bred man, but he had an air of sadness. Perhaps with exaggerated familiarity—God should

---

The novelist, short-story writer, and playwright DINO BUZZATI *(1906–1972) was born in Belluno and spent much of his life in Milan. From 1928 until his death, he worked as a journalist for the* Corriere della Sera. *Best known for his Kafkaesque novel,* The Tartar Steppe *(1940), Buzzati wrote many stories that represent the unsettling eruption of fantastic incidents in everyday life. Several selections have been published in English, including* Catastrophe *(1966) and* Restless Nights *(1983).*

have stopped me—I complimented him on his elegance; and I even dared to ask him who his tailor might be.

He smiled curiously, as if he had expected my question. "Nearly no one knows him," he said. "Still, he's a great master. And he works only when the work comes to him. For a few initiates."

"So that I couldn't . . . ?"

"Oh, try, try. His name is Corticella—Alfonso Corticella—via Ferrara 17."

"He will be expensive, I imagine."

"I believe so, but I swear I don't know. He made me this suit three years ago, and he still hasn't sent me the bill."

"Corticella? Via Ferrara 17, did you say?"

"Exactly," the stranger answered. And he left me to join another group of people.

At via Ferrara 17, I found a house like so many others and like those of so many other tailors; it was the residence of Alfonso Corticella. It was he who came to let me in. He was a little old man with black hair, which was, however, obviously dyed.

To my surprise, he was not hard to deal with. In fact, he seemed eager for me to become his customer. I explained to him how I had gotten his address, praised his cutting, and asked him to make me a suit. We selected a gray wool, then he took my measurements and offered to come to my apartment for the fitting. I asked him the price. There was no hurry, he answered, we could always come to an agreement. What a congenial man, I thought at first. Nevertheless, later, while I was returning home, I realized that the little old man had left me feeling uneasy (perhaps because of his too warm and persistent smiles). In short, I had no desire at all to see him again. But now the suit had been ordered. And after about three weeks it was ready.

When they brought it to me, I tried it on in front of a mirror for a little while. It was a masterpiece. Yet, I don't know why, perhaps because of my memory of the unpleasant old man, I didn't have any desire to wear it. And weeks passed before I decided to do so.

That day I shall remember forever. It was a Tuesday in April and it was raining. When I had slipped into the clothes—jacket, trousers, and vest—I was pleased to observe that they didn't pull and weren't tight anywhere, as almost always happens with new suits. And yet they hugged my body perfectly.

As a rule I put nothing in the right jacket pocket; in the left one, I keep my cards. This explains why, only after a couple of hours at the office, casually slipping my hand into the right pocket, I noticed that there was a piece of paper inside. Was it maybe the tailor's bill?

No. It was a ten thousand lire note.

I was astounded. I certainly had not put it there. On the other hand, it was absurd to think it a joke of the tailor Corticella. Much less did it seem a gift from my maid, the only person, other than the tailor, who had occasion to go near my suit. Or was it a counterfeit note? I looked at it in the light, I compared it to others. It was no different from these.

There was a single possible explanation—Corticella's absentmindedness. Perhaps a customer had come to make a payment. The tailor didn't have his wallet with him just then, and so to avoid leaving the money around, he slipped it into my jacket, which was hanging on a mannequin. These things can happen.

I rang for my secretary. I wanted to write a letter to Corticella, returning the money. But (and I can't say why I did it) I slipped my hand into the pocket again.

"Is anything wrong, sir? Do you feel ill?" asked my secretary, who entered at that moment. I must have turned pale as death. In my pocket my fingers touched the edge of another strip of paper, which had not been there a few minutes before.

"No, no, it's nothing," I said. "A slight dizziness. It happens to me sometimes. Maybe I'm a little tired. You can go now, dear. I wanted to dictate a letter, but we'll do it later."

Only after my secretary had gone did I dare remove the piece of paper from my pocket. It was another ten thousand lire note. Then I tried a third time. And a third banknote appeared.

My heart began to race. I had the feeling that for some mysterious reason I was involved in the plot of a fairy tale, like those that are told to children and no one believes are true.

On the pretext that I was not feeling well, I left the office and went home. I needed to be alone. Luckily, my maid had already gone. I shut the doors, lowered the blinds. I began to take out the notes one after another, very quickly. My pocket seemed inexhaustible.

I worked in a spasmodic nervous tension, fearing that the miracle might stop at any moment. I wanted it to continue all day and night, until I had accumulated billions. But at a certain point the flow diminished.

Before me stood an impressive heap of banknotes. The important thing now was to hide them, so no one would get wind of the affair. I emptied an old trunk full of rugs and put the money, arranged in many little piles, at the bottom. Then I slowly began counting. There were 58 million lire.

I awoke the next morning after the maid arrived. She was amazed to find me in bed still completely dressed. I tried to laugh, explaining that I had drunk a little too much the night before and sleep had suddenly seized me.

A new anxiety arose: she asked me to take off the suit, so she could at least give it a brushing.

I answered that I had to go out immediately and didn't have time to change. Then I hurried to a store selling ready-to-wear clothes to buy another suit made of a similar material; I would leave this one in the maid's care. "Mine," the suit that in the course of a few days would make me one of the most powerful men in the world, I would hide in a safe place.

I didn't know whether I was living in a dream, whether I was happy or suffocating under the burden of an arduous fate. On the street, I was continually feeling the magic pocket through my raincoat. Each time I breathed a sigh of relief. Beneath the cloth answered the comforting crackle of paper money.

But a singular coincidence cooled my joyous delirium. News of a robbery that occurred the day before headlined the morning papers. A bank's armored car, after making the rounds of the branches, had been carrying the day's deposits to the main office when it was seized and cleaned out in viale Palmanova by four criminals. As people swarmed around the scene, one of the gangsters began to shoot to keep them away. A passerby was killed. But, above all, the amount of the loot struck me: it was exactly 58 million—like the money I had put in the trunk.

Could there be a connection between my sudden wealth and the criminal raid that had happened almost simultaneously? It seemed foolish to think so. What's more, I am not generally superstitious. All the same, the incident left me very confused.

The more one gets, the more one wants. I was already rich, considering my modest habits. But the illusion of a life of unlimited luxury was compelling. And that same evening I set to work again. Now I proceeded more slowly, with less torture to my nerves. Another 135 million was added to my previous treasure.

That night I couldn't close my eyes. Was it the presentiment of danger? Or the tormented conscience of one who undeservedly wins a fabulous fortune? Or was it a kind of confused remorse? At dawn I leaped from the bed, dressed, and ran outside to get a newspaper.

As I read, I lost my breath. A terrible fire, which had begun in a naphtha warehouse, had half-destroyed a building on the main street, via San Cloro. The flames had consumed, among other things, the safes of a large real estate company which contained more than 130 million in cash. Two firemen had met their deaths in the blaze.

Should I now, perhaps, list my crimes one by one? Yes, because now I knew that the money the jacket gave me came from those crimes, from blood, from desperation and death, from hell. But I was caught within the snare of reason, which scornfully refused to allow me to admit that I could be in any way responsible. And then the temptation resumed, then the hand—it was so easy!—slipped into the pocket, and the fingers, with the quickest delight, grasped the edges of always another banknote. The money, the divine money!

Without moving out of my old apartment (so as not to attract attention), I soon bought a huge villa, owned a precious collection of paintings, drove around in luxurious automobiles, and having left my firm for "reasons of health," traveled back and forth throughout the world in the company of marvelous women.

I knew that whenever I drew money from the jacket, something base and painful happened in the world. But it was still always a vague awareness, not supported by logical proofs. Meanwhile, at each new collection, my conscience was degraded, becoming more and more vile. And the tailor? I telephoned him to ask for the bill, but no one answered. In via Ferrara, where I went to search for him, they told me that he had emigrated abroad, they didn't know where. Everything then conspired to show me that without knowing it, I had bound myself in a pact with the Devil.

Then, one morning, in the building where I had lived for many years, they found a sixty-year-old retired woman asphyxiated by gas; she had killed herself for having mislaid her monthly pension of 30 thousand lire, which she had collected the day before (and which had ended up in my hands).

Enough, enough! In order not to sink to the depths of the abyss, I had to rid myself of the jacket. And not by surrendering it to someone else, because the horror would continue (who would ever be able to resist such enticement?). Its destruction was absolutely necessary.

By car I arrived at a secluded valley in the Alps. I left the car in a grassy clearing and set out in the direction of the forest. There wasn't a living soul in sight. Having gone beyond the forest, I reached the rocky ground of the moraine. Here, between two gigantic boulders, I pulled the wicked jacket from a knapsack, sprinkled it with kerosene, and lit it. In a few minutes only ashes were left.

But at the last flicker of the flames, behind me—it seemed about two or three meters away—a human voice resounded, "Too late, too late!" Terrified, I turned around with a serpent's snap. But I saw no one. I explored the area, jumping from one huge rock to another, to hunt out the damned person. Nothing. There were only rocks.

Notwithstanding the fright I experienced, I went back down to the base of the valley with a feeling of relief. I was free at last. And rich, luckily.

But my car was no longer in the grassy clearing. And after I returned to the city, my sumptuous villa had disappeared; in its place was an uncultivated field with some poles that bore the notice Municipal Land For Sale. My savings accounts were also completely drained, but I couldn't explain how. The big packets of deeds in my numerous safe-deposit boxes had vanished too. And there was dust, nothing but dust, in the old trunk.

I now resumed working with difficulty, I can hardly get through a day, and what is stranger, no one seems to be amazed by my sudden ruin.

And I know that it's still not over. I know that one day my doorbell will ring, and I'll answer it to find that cursed tailor before me, with his contemptible smile, asking for the final settling of my account.

(1966)

Deep Water

Marilia Mazzeo

SO WHEN WILL YOU COME BACK? I asked her. She said nothing, no answer, just a brief silence, feigned inattention, as if she hadn't heard the question. I listened to her faint breathing over the phone against the shrill wail of the vacuum cleaner someone was running in her apartment. Then she hurriedly started to talk about something else, a science fiction movie she'd seen last night. I told her I don't like science fiction.

She phoned to tell me she wouldn't be coming to work today because of the deep water. I said, Don't you have boots? She answered no. This strikes me as a silly excuse, I said. Why don't you buy them? She told me that where she lives, Salute, there aren't any shops, she'd have to go to Accademia, but she can't get there because the water's almost a meter deep. I offered to buy her a pair of boots and bring them to her tonight, so at least tomorrow she could come to the studio. She said it didn't matter. She said

Born in 1972 in Ravenna, MARILIA MAZZEO *studied architecture in Venice. This story, her first appearance in English, is the title piece of a 1998 collection in which she represents the lives of several university students.*

she hates the deep water, and when it's there she shuts herself up at home and doesn't even look out the windows because it makes her anxious and she feels as if she's slowly sinking, together with the city, into the lagoon. She asked me to explain to Siviero why she isn't coming today. I reminded her she's stayed home lots of times recently because she had the flu. She said never mind.

I'm at the studio by myself. The three of us work here and Siviero hasn't yet returned from his lunch break. I don't find it particularly easy to greet him with "Marcella phoned to say she can't come." He'll start cursing. He isn't pleased with Marcella, and he isn't entirely wrong. I feel I'm to blame, because I was the one who brought her here. I'm sitting by the phone and can't get on with my work. I don't know why the call to Marcella has filled me with worry and sadness.

I don't believe her. I suddenly realize I don't believe her anymore. Deep water can be an excuse not to come to work; so can the flu. Yet on days when she said she was sick, I actually met her on the street. Glad to see her, I asked, Better already? No, no, she answered, looking around, frightened, I still have a fever, but I had to go out to buy myself something to eat. That time too I offered to do the shopping and bring it to her. I even scolded her because you don't go around with a fever, but she said no thanks, I'll do the best I can, she kissed me on the cheek and dashed off in a hurry. She had nothing in her hands. She didn't look like someone who'd caught a cold; her face just looked a bit tired and rundown, and there were some circles round her eyes.

I think Marcella wants to get fired. I'm not sure but I

feel it, I feel it as you feel winter coming, I feel it more strongly with every passing moment. I could be wrong and Marcella might be sincere and simply have no boots. But I remember she once talked to me about being fired. It was perhaps two months ago. We left the studio together and were walking, worn out. She said she was thinking about her situation, working at a graphics studio, and perhaps it'd be better to quit. You could've knocked me over with a feather. I don't understand why, I told her. There are so many reasons, she muttered confusedly. Well, what reasons? I insisted. She fetched a deep sigh. School, she said finally, I can't find enough time to study for my courses, four hours a day is a lot for someone who's going to university. You don't understand because you don't go.

In reality I'm doing many more things than she is. Every morning I go to the academy and every afternoon I stay at the studio till eight; on Saturdays and Sundays I also work at my cousin's pizzeria, which is no joke. I never have any free time. Until recently, if I ever had some free time, I'd spend it with Marcella, talking. For instance, that night she was tired and wanted to stop working, I brought her home with me, heated up two frozen pizzas for supper, and we talked forever. We talk quite easily together. We have lots in common. We have the same ideas about everything. But I'm thinking I should say "we had," because now I feel everything is changing.

I was the one who brought her here and asked Siviero to hire her. I met Marcella last year at Ciro's house, when he hadn't yet moved to the area around Palazzo Carminati and was living in a hovel near the Gesuiti church, although a rather delightful hovel, where he often invited us to drink wine and look at his paintings. Marcella had somehow turned up in the midst of these people from the academy. She'd just arrived from Viterbo to sign up for the course in architecture. I asked her, How on earth did you wind up in Venice, then, and not Rome? She explained to me that in Italy there are a limited number of places in universities, and you have to try the admission exam everywhere and wherever they take you they take you: she had taken it at Venice. Then she asked why someone like me from Rijeka—it's really called Rijeka and not Fiume as they say here—doesn't go to the academy in Zagreb or Ljubljana. I in turn explained to her that nothing's going on there— everyone who can crosses the border, and luckily for me I have a cousin here who lets me work in his pizzeria. Then I told her I was looking for an artisanal graphics studio, the kind that exists only in Venice, with no computer graphics because I detest computers, but rather one of those old printing shops where they make engravings, lithographs, etchings, and so forth, and I might've found it because just around that time I'd gone to speak with some professors at the school of graphic art and they'd sent me to Siviero. Marcella listened to me very attentively and actually every- one listened to me that night; Marcella agreed with me while the others contradicted me—they said the computer possesses creative possibilities that remain unexplored and so forth, besides three guys in their last year at the acad- emy built an installation that combined broken televisions, spray cans, parts from electronic keyboards, and coca cola cans and then they poured acrylic paint over it, so I didn't think they'd be sensitive to the charm of an acquatint. But Marcella was sensitive to it, and she too detests computers. She told me she would also like to work in Siviero's printing shop. So she gave me her phone number that night, and after a month we both wound up in this studio, where Siviero started to print those postcards for cultivated tourists, assorted views of bridges, canals, and cats sitting on wells with sewn bindings and embossed covers—the only work that earns him a living because these Venetian images sell like bread—while he prints his own pieces and those of other artists and shows them in his little gallery facing the Fenice. He pays us 250 euros a month and little by little teaches us to do all the rest. It's such an enjoyable job, I just don't understand why Marcella doesn't want to do it anymore. I feel as if she's lost the desire for it. In winter we froze to death because the print shop is a huge warehouse, cold and damp, full of wonders like a wizard's castle but cold, with no other heating than a small gas stove where we'd all go to thaw our hands. Marcella would come to the studio bundled up in layers of sweaters, her cheeks red from the cold. She always listened to me with such a sweet smile. She would always say, That's exactly what I've always thought—since my art school days. I'd laugh, because she had just left art school the year before. I'd go back to work, and she would stay there, her hands over the grate in the stove, because Marcella is lazy, sensitive to cold and lazy. She's going to school less and less, I know it, and if she stops working, I don't think she'll go more often or study more. Perhaps I just don't understand, but I see students always talking about how much work they have and how tremendously stressful the university is, and then I always see them at the San Stin bar sitting around, doing nothing.

From the beginning, for instance, I'd stay here till late at night in order to print my drawings, and I used to encourage Marcella to do the same, because Marcella is clever and creative—I know it—and she has lots of material she can work on. But she nearly always says she doesn't have the time. She draws small, strange fairy-tale landscapes, which seem like they're from another planet and bear no resemblance to anything else. Marcella has great imagination and talent and no one knows how she ended up in that faculty, which isn't in the least creative. If I've understood correctly, it's a stubborn attempt to join the most unlike things, like the Kantian sublime and construction theory, the modernist avant-gardes and urban-planning legislation, reinforced concrete and ancient Greece, all inside the same cauldron from which will emerge a profession that no one can really identify. I told Marcella to read Ruskin, and she's been enthusiastic about Ruskin. I told her the story of Bauhaus, and she's been enthusiastic about Bauhaus. I even told her, Pack in the university, and we'll learn artisanal graphics better so that in a few years we can set up our own printing shop, something refined for artists and connoisseurs, and we might even make money because all the other shops will have finally gone over to the computer and it'll be impossible to find someone who can hold a pen in his hand. Marcella said it was a wonderful idea and she'd have a think about it.

I can't move away from the phone because I feel like calling her back. I can't convince myself that she's become inattentive and distant, that she no longer tells me frankly what she's thinking. We were such friends until recently. She would phone me at midnight to tell me about a great film she'd just seen. With me she was always so pleasant and agreeable that I thought perhaps, if we continued to be such friends, we might even wind up together, possibly get married. We certainly wouldn't have had lots of money but perhaps we could rent a one-room apartment. We would've had children as well—tall, slender, pale with dark hair that was always tousled, just like Marcella and me, since we resemble one another as if we were brother and sister. But it was better if I stopped thinking because she started seeing Giacomo and didn't even let me know; one night he just came to the studio to pick her up and I saw them holding hands as they left. Giacomo is an older guy, around thirty, from the architecture course; he has a beard that looks like chafed straw and a facial expression that's always dark and sarcastic—he isn't handsome at all. I asked Marcella where she came across this Giacomo. She said she met him at Trefori's funeral. And who's this Trefori? I wondered. Where have you been? she said. Are you pulling my leg?

No, I can't phone her now. I feel as if the tide of deep water were slowly dragging Marcella away from me. And yet I don't believe she and Giacomo talk as easily as we used to talk. Perhaps Marcella is doing the right thing to get fired, perhaps she's realized she wants to be an architect and nothing else. But then why was she so enthusiastic before and where did her enthusiasm go, her passion for Cinquecento engravings and Egon Schiele's drawings, which we went to see together at the graphic arts museum in Vienna, and what happened to her collection of stamps for sealing wax, which took us so often to the antique stalls? Where do things wind up when people suddenly change?

This is why her phone call hurt me, I think, much more than that time I saw her holding hands with Giacomo. It hurt me so much I still can't move away from the phone. I'd like to stand up and get on with my work; I have to clean the press, prepare the oil-based inks by mixing in some magnesium powder, dissolve the flakes of shellac in alcohol and soak the heavy paper, otherwise Siviero will really get angry. But I keep on sitting here, even if I understand that calling her back is impossible and useless, it's useless to tell her I understand everything even if she doesn't want to say anything to me anymore, I understand she no longer cares at all about graphic art and our projects and perhaps even those strange tiny landscapes. I can't phone her, because there's nothing you can do about the deep water, you can only keep on watching and hoping it doesn't cause too much damage.

(1998)

Built to Kill

Tiziano Scarpa

"THE FIRST SUICIDE dates back to Friday the 15th of June, between four and six in the morning."

"Or so the report concluded."

"Medical examiners are not inclined to take wild guesses. Or do we wish, Inspector, to cast aspersions on your colleagues from the outset?"

"Not on your life, Dr. Hoffmann, especially seeing as how you too are my colleague . . . And I'll bet you'll stay that way for the time being, given the m.o. of this case."

"All these cases, I would say."

"Hold your horses, Doctor . . . We're dealing with this one right now."

"The victim hanged himself from a statue on the facade of the Church of the Scalzi."

Born in Venice in 1963, TIZIANO SCARPA *now lives in Milan. During the 1990s he was associated with the emerging writers dubbed the "cannibals" because of their interest in subcultural experiences and popular genres like the thriller. Scarpa has published a novel, stories, and essays, in addition to an unconventional guidebook,* Venice Is a Fish *(2000). This piece, first performed as a play on RadioRai in 1997, constitutes his debut in English.*

"It'd just been restored."

"They had removed the scaffolding two days before. Cleaning the blackened stones required years. Then there was the task of reinforcing the structural elements, but in the end the church has been returned to its Baroque magnificence."

"A breathtaking sight."

"Bear in mind, Inspector, that this monument is the first to loom before tourists when they exit the train station; they are obliged to pass by it as soon as they set foot in the city."

"The corpse, anyhow, was hanging from a rope tied around a saint's neck."

"As if he had wished to personify a type of human failure suspended from an incomparable model. The corpse of a mortal hanging from the incorruptible statue of a saint!"

"And so, Doctor, according to your theory—"

"According to my theory, the choice of hanging and the site of the suicide—the very threshold of the city for foreigners—enclose a message that is crystal clear."

"'A horrific toll to beauty,'" you've written, "'to be paid by whoever enters Venice.'"

"Precisely. You are much more conscientious than my pupils, Inspector. You recall my conclusions verbatim."

"Let's proceed to the second case."

"The second case, in my view, presents a symbolic elaboration that is even more complex. Of course, suicide is always a form of communication."

"Even when someone kills himself without leaving a note?"

"Indeed. Self-destruction is an extreme statement that

the subject could not utter in any other fashion. It seems that to do away with oneself may be less difficult than to express the terrible truth of one's condition."

"This time the suicide chained his ankles and wrists to a mooring post in the Canal Grande."

"The night of May 9th. Precisely. He apparently waited for the sea to rise and completely submerge him. He allowed himself to die by drowning. What a frightful death!"

"Rather imaginative as well."

"I think it highly improper, Inspector, to take this as an occasion to pour our cynicism on the pitiful dead."

"You mean *my* cynicism. Forgive me, sir, but I thought dispassionate science delighted in appreciating the pitiless aspects of reality."

"You have a rather quaint notion of us scientists. But I am not the topic of this discussion. Returning to our second misadventure, note that the mooring post in question is located—"

"Close to a pier at the Ca' d'Oro. Another recently restored monument."

"I am reminded of an old patient of mine, another Venetian who committed suicide in analogous circumstances several years ago."

"Did you know him well?"

"I would say virtually not at all. He had been entrusted to my care scarcely three days before his death."

"Too late even for a sorcerer!"

"Indeed, Inspector. Obviously I could not delude myself that I had found some reason for him to continue living. To be perfectly honest, I didn't even have sufficient time to comprehend the real motive for his self-destructive impulses."

"But you were able to examine his papers after the fact."

"Members of the family granted me access to a diary. Upon reading it, I discovered that the man had been obsessed by the beauty of Venice. This city afforded him a feeling of unbearable suffocation."

"A sort of Stendhal syndrome."

"Not quite. That's pop psychology. Besides, you should not confuse an occasional indigestion of beauty with a permanent intoxication. The Stendhal syndrome tends to be experienced by those ill-equipped tourists who have left behind the ugliness of their suburbs, where developments continue to be built like so many cemeteries for the living dead. It almost goes without saying that upon arriving in Venice an individual accustomed to that kind of landscape will feel faint. He is evidently incapable of enduring the massive doses of beauty that the city hurls at him all in one go. But would he then be moved to take his life? Come now, Inspector, no one would stop him from packing his bags and returning to swallow a healthy mouthful of dirty air amongst his beloved exhaust pipes."

"While a resident of Venice—"

"A resident of Venice must shoulder the burden of this enormous aesthetic weight for his entire life. That old patient of mine felt like a mouse in a trap, strangled by the charm of streets a meter wide. These narrow calli allow your sight no escape, they squeeze it between a pictorial foreshortening and an architectural epiphany; they crush your eyes between the grace of a bridge and the shady charm of a portico."

"Not by chance, then, was he found in——"

"Calle del Paradiso, the most evocative street in Venice."

"The bas reliefs on the triangular architrave, the exposed beams jutting out from the buttresses . . . It is very beautiful indeed, perhaps even the most beautiful of all."

"But for him, clearly, the most lethal."

"Here too there had been restoration work. The calle was reopened to foot traffic just a short while before."

"In fact, all three cases present us with monuments that had remained covered for some time, a detail that rendered them more tolerable, so to speak, more human. When the scaffolding and platforms were removed, however, for these already vexed individuals it was as if an aesthetic tide had regained its original force, utterly overwhelming the dykes . . . Each of them received a coup de grace from the beauty."

"But, Doctor, the man who was found in Calle del Paradiso had been poisoned."

"Yes, but the city itself had administered the true poison."

"Hence, in your view, Venice would be some sort of serial murderer."

"You do me the honor of citing a phrase—deliberately, I recognize—that has had a certain echo in the media. In reality, that fortunate expression appeared in a passage from a much more articulate scientific report."

"Which gave you no small satisfaction at the international psychiatric conference in Pittsburgh last spring."

"That report was actually quite a success with my transatlantic colleagues."

"It has also established you as one of the most original

psychotherapists now working. After a career that had been—if you will permit me—rather less distinguished."

"On the contrary, Inspector. Unlike members of the police force, we have no need of recommendations to win appointments and obtain promotions."

"Is that so?"

"My trajectory as a scholar and therapist has always been characterized by the most scrupulous professionalism. I do not see what other parameters you may have at your disposal to evaluate the quality of—"

"Yes, yes, but I'm not talking about your career as a shrink. As a young man, before specializing in psychiatry, you set out on another path. My suspicions were aroused by all those technical references to building, all those architectural metaphors in your report. You're a failed architect, Dr. Hoffmann."

"How can you say that?"

"I discovered it in my spare time, between requests for recommendations. I came across several old articles of yours. The ones where you try to demonstrate the absurdity of any type of restoration, where you go so far as to propose a systematic demolition of historic buildings just to solve the problem in the most radical way."

"I don't understand what you're getting at."

"Worried? I remember your essay on the campanile of San Marco, which collapsed at the beginning of the twentieth century and was reconstructed by Venetians who followed the principle of *as it was, where it was*. 'The thought of rebuilding something that might be only remotely connected to the original is sheer folly. One might as well raze it to the ground.' Do I misquote you, Doctor?"

"You're quoting things I wrote so many years ago."

"And what about your euphoric comments when the Teatro La Fenice burned? 'I am not afraid of being the only person to rejoice amidst so many hypocrites who rend their clothing in grief. Finally, an important building must be reconstructed *ex novo*. I hope that this city's funereal obsession does not lead to the insane plan of rebuilding the theater just as it was. Let us put an end to our slavery to the dead; let us sever our bonds to the decayed aesthetic of our ancestors. They certainly didn't hesitate to do so! Did they perhaps respect the Gothic? Neoclassicism? Would we have the Baroque if the seventeenth century had lapsed into a scholastic imitation of the Renaissance? The burning of La Fenice has renewed the promise of a Futurist utopia!'"

"Inspector, these are the exaggerations of journalists. Never trust the quotations in their interviews. I am, in any case, no longer an architect."

"It is actually Venice's fault that you never became one. You hate this city; you have never forgiven her for her palaces and canals, calli and piazzas, churches and porticoes. At seven, you were brought here from Berlin; you were raised in a place engulfed by monuments, churches, historic buildings. A city where no space exists to build anything, where one can only restore, renovate, redecorate, respect the old, venerate the ancient, worship the decrepit. A city where one must forgo the expression of something truly new, instead of leaving a trace as in any other city in the world, instead of marking one's passage on the earth with one's own little milestone."

"Do you realize what you're saying? What you describe would be an unbearable situation for an architect."

"A situation that could lead to madness. Or even to a projection of it onto others. Through a twist of fate, your native city has recently been transformed into a permanent construction site. When you finally realized that your Berlin had become an architect's paradise, entire districts demolished and redesigned—"

"Potsdamerplatz made over from the top down, cheerfully distorted—"

"You couldn't bear it. You killed three men who had nothing to fear from the beauty of the stones of Venice. You portrayed them as victims of a self-destructive aesthetic obsession. You went so far as to theorize a new psychopathology, winning celebrity at your victims' expense. You became the darling of contractors who want to get rich quick with substandard housing; you furnished arguments and justifications for the worst kinds of building speculation. Above all, you took revenge on Venice, accusing her of being the most ruthless serial killer of her own inhabitants.

"You may phone your lawyer, Dr. Hoffmann."

(2000)

Enchantment

Mario Rigoni Stern

LORENZO HAD WORKED at the sawmill ever since he was a boy, and he had grown up, one might say, amongst timber and lumber. The wood formed part of his life, and the resin had even impregnated his skin. When, near the end of the day, the wagons arrived from the communal forests laden with logs, he was quick to unload them: he skillfully harpooned them with his hooked pole and rolled them over the barriers onto the stacks in the clearing before the mill.

In the evening, when the saw had finished its continuous alternating movements and stood silent, when the water from the millrace had been diverted, and the last boards had been set on the racks, checked for levelness, and separated by wedges of the right thickness, Lorenzo stayed to clean the sawing machinery, sweep the floor, and make

MARIO RIGONI STERN *was born in 1921 in Asiago, where he lives. During World War II, he fought in the Italian army at various fronts, Albanian and Greek, French and Russian. Upon Italy's fall, he was captured by the Germans and imprisoned in concentration camps. These experiences, along with daily life in the Veneto, form the basis of his moving memoirs and stories. Available in English are* The Sergeant in the Snow *(1953) and* The Story of Tönle *(1979).*

certain that every tool was in its place. He finally locked the huge doors and consigned the keys to the owner's hands. He lifted his beret, white with sawdust, and said good-bye. "See you tomorrow."

In the morning, he was always the first to arrive. During June and July the sun illuminated the racks of boards, and the wholesome smell of wood filled the air; during December and January the valley was still dark, only the highest peaks beginning to brighten, and the snow that had fallen on the timber and lumber, as on the forest, wrapped nature in its mantle. The smoke from the chimneys dispersed with the sun's arrival, but the smell remained in the air.

As soon as Lorenzo reached the mill, he went to check the temperature on the thermometer and then approached the owner to ask for the keys.

"Buongiorno. Here we go, another day."

"Buongiorno, Lorenzo. How many degrees?" When he heard the reply, he would always say, "It isn't as cold as it used to be." Then he stood up from his desk to stoke the fire in the stove.

Lorenzo unlocked the doors, let in the water from the millrace, set the paddle wheel turning, and tested the mechanism that put the saw in motion. Meanwhile the sawyer and two senior workers arrived.

According to the owner's instructions and on the basis of the orders and the inventory, Lorenzo set the distance of the blades to obtain the right thickness: for planks of sixty, fifty, and forty centimeters; for boards of thirty, twenty-five, and fifteen; for beams, rafters, and joists. It was always Lorenzo who chose the logs suited to the need;

and the saw would start cutting up down up down up down, forming heaps of sawdust.

Tireless and agile, Lorenzo handled the logs as if they were twigs, he used the hook to align them next to the saw, and with a sure eye he set them in the right position so as to produce the least waste when they were trimmed. Sometimes the sawyer adjusted them a centimeter or so. Together they secured the log on the feeding track, and then with a movement of his hand the sawyer shifted the rod that set going the alternating movement of the blades and the forward movement of the track.

As the log reached the end and the boards started to split apart at the top, Lorenzo grabbed one after the other and, with the flat of his hand, dusted them off to examine the cut and the beauty of the grain. Then he passed them to the two senior workers who carried them away on a cart to set on the racks in the open air, allowing the wood to season and become serviceable for the work of carpenters and craftsmen.

He was a man of few words. Besides, work like this didn't require many words. The important thing was to observe before making a decision and use one's strength intelligently by lifting with the proper tools. And then too the job was in his blood: his grandfather as well as his father had worked at the sawmill, with the current owner's grandfather and father.

Late one summer morning, while he was working with the hook as usual, shifting and choosing logs for the saw, moving with the grace of a goat and the strength of a bull, he felt an intense stare and turned his head. The eyes of a young woman were directed at his. Deeper than the night sky, brighter than the sun on the snow, moist like those of a young doe. He stood motionless, his hook attached to the log, feeling his legs weaken and his arms become paralyzed. Until she disengaged her gaze from his face, shifting it to the legs inside his corduroy trousers. At that moment, with a force that he had never before exerted, he succeeded in turning himself round to make the log roll over. But he still felt those eyes on his back, as he adroitly contrived to arrange the wood on the saw table; and when he decided a moment later to look at her a second time, he saw that she was beautiful, very beautiful. Her body was slender and erect, she flaunted her chest, her long black hair fell to her shoulders. Again he felt his legs weaken, and his heart filled with tumult. The girl smiled at him and drew away, proud.

Lorenzo went home for the midday meal. He ate indifferently, unaware of what his mother had put on his plate. She asked him if he weren't feeling well. "I have a headache," he replied. And it was true, since he felt as if two drumsticks were beating on his forehead. He rose from the table without finishing his meal and went to sit beneath the thorn tree to smoke a hand-rolled cigarette. Yet not even the cigarette gave him pleasure, and it went out immediately. He was thinking, but about what he couldn't say exactly—about his vague malaise, about those eyes that kept appearing before him and took away his will.

In the afternoon he resumed working, yet with the constant fear and desire that she might return. Luckily, but also unfortunately, the day ended without her reappearance. Lorenzo diverted the water from the millrace, cleaned the sawing machinery, swept the floor, checked whether every tool was in its place, locked the doors, and consigned the keys to the owner. "See you tomorrow," said the owner, who remained with the keys in hand, bewildered, because this was the first time that Lorenzo had left without saying goodbye.

Lorenzo did not wash in the fountain in the courtyard before entering his house, he did not remove his boots to put on his cloth slippers, he did not sit at the table for supper. He did not respond to his mother's questions. He went out to walk through the streets of the village, in the center, around the hotels, hoping to meet her, to see her eyes again and find that they were different from what he remembered. Because, of course, those eyes could exist only in his imagination. She was only a vacationer who had arrived from the city, he told himself; perhaps she had traveled from very far away. Yes, she was certainly a witch. A malign witch who had come from who knows where to cast a spell on him, to ruin him. A creature of evil who had reappeared on the earth.

When it was pitch dark, he returned home and went straight up to his room, although not to sleep. Always those eyes, always that figure. He fell asleep near dawn and dreamed that she was begging him to make love. He awoke confused. He managed to formulate a thought. "She has bewitched me." He ate breakfast listlessly, without appetite. He set off for the mill. His work went badly: the hook felt heavy, the logs too heavy, the boards didn't turn out well, he didn't hear what the sawyer said to him. The morning passed without her reappearance, and it seemed as if the spell were abating, even if slowly.

The heat grew stifling in the afternoon; a storm was rolling through the mountains, and thunder could be heard fading in the valleys. "When will this weather break?" the workers wondered, with the sultriness sticking to their skin. Yet the storm withdrew without bringing any relief, in fact only increasing the heavy humid heat. Before dusk three wagons arrived with timber to be shifted to the stacks. The workers slipped off the chains that held the logs bound together and started to unload them. Then she reappeared. Lorenzo immediately felt her eyes on his neck. He tried to resist, tried not to turn round to look at her, but he couldn't for very long and turned just a little. The others didn't notice his state of mind and told him, "Get moving so we can go home. Pay attention to those logs—you might break a leg." The owner, whose sons were watching the wagons being unloaded, told them, "Lorenzo doesn't look well." That evening Lorenzo again left the mill without saying goodbye to anyone.

As on the night before he walked through the village streets and piazzas, hoping and fearing that he might meet her. In the morning he returned to the mill, and after an hour the sawyer told the owner, "Something's up with Lorenzo. He's straining to do what he used to do so easily."

"Tomorrow morning," thought the owner, "instead of keeping him here at the mill I'll send him to the forest in Pian del Rio to mark up the prime grade lumber. This way he can take a break and let his mind wander." When the time came to stop work, the owner called him and said, "Early tomorrow the drivers are going to pick up timber at that parcel in Pian del Rio. Why don't you go with them and choose the best cuts? There's no hurry to come back."

"Very well," replied Lorenzo. "Tomorrow morning at five. I'll be on time."

The following day they traveled the white road, climbing toward the forest with tie-rods and chains. The horses clambered like goats. Lorenzo seemed to be sleepwalking, since that night too she had appeared to him in a dream. When they arrived at the plot of timber, he had to immerse his head in the Rio's cold water to regain the lucidity needed to select the logs that the owner wanted and mark them for the drivers.

After his work was done, he rode the piebald down to the track where they had left the wagons. He suddenly found himself before her again, in a clearing, where she was gathering bilberries. She was with some other people. They were laughing, joking. She greeted him by name.

"Ciao, Lorenzo."

He felt his legs give, all his strength slip away, his heart burst. Trembling, he freed himself from her gaze and ran off into the forest like a frightened deer, pursued by a pack of howling dogs.

From that time onward his condition grew worse. He lost his appetite, couldn't sleep. He no longer had the strength to work. The owner told him to go to the doctor, and the doctor gave him a month off for "nervous exhaustion." Then another fifteen days. Lorenzo told someone that a witch, beautiful yet pitiless, had cast a spell on him.

That autumn I had to go to collect the wood that I had been granted by municipal law. They had assigned me a lot in a remote, inconvenient area that bordered on another commune, and I asked the foresters if they could recommend someone who might give me a hand. "Lorenzo can do it," they said. "You'd also be doing him a favor because he can use some company." And so I asked him.

The following morning Lorenzo joined me in the forest and started to work with the axe, creating a stack of wood and carrying it to a spot that a wagon could reach. He did at least twice the work I did, and I told him to take it easy because the forest is greedy.

"You seem fit to me."

"Yes," he replied, "the evil eye is leaving me. The witch is giving it to someone else."

At noon he lit a fire to heat the polenta to eat with the soppressata and cheese. He ate with gusto and, during an hour's break, as he smoked a cigarette, he told me this story.

(1998)

Music Lessons

Claudio Magris

THE MAESTRO STOPPED a moment to observe the villa, which at this point was fairly close by. He was panting a little, a little more than the moderate slope of the road required. He had inadvertently fallen into the habit of panting unnecessarily every so often, a minor mania that his body suddenly demanded, like old men who yield to caprice and willfulness, slight anticipations and compensations in their vast disagreement with reality. He could already see the gate, the spiral curves of its wrought-iron bars intertwined with the shapes of repeated garlands of violets, and the veranda blanketed by creeping plants in front of the sitting room, where Vilardi was probably waiting for him. In fact, it was Maestro Vilardi, who now had more right to this title than he, Salman Meierstein, esteemed teacher at the conservatory.

He had traveled that road many times by car. The

CLAUDIO MAGRIS *was born in 1939 in Trieste, where he lives and teaches at the university. A literary critic as well as a fiction writer, he is a subtle stylist who has devoted his attention to central and eastern European themes. Several of his books have appeared in English, including* Danube *(1986) and* Microcosms *(1997).*

signora used to send the chauffeur to collect him. The huge black automobile would ascend the road cut halfway up the hill, high above the boundless sea, and enter the park. In those days, a servant escorted him to the sitting room, the pupil offered him a soft, moist hand, the servant returned with coffee and the signora, who lingered a couple of minutes and spoke of her husband, the senator long deceased, and of the lands and estates and country houses in Friuli, so utterly different from that villa in the city. Then she left him alone with her son, for the lesson. The young man would lift his violin and begin to play. Salman listened, his eyes half-closed, nodded his approval at several lovely staccatos, recognized in various passages the eager execution he now knew quite well. Occasionally, there would be an extraordinary flash, which gleamed and vanished like lightning amid so many familiar things, grazing him with a painful contraction. Then he intervened, corrected, suggested several ingenious bow movements which had crossed his mind, a more intense vibrato or a deeper touch he recalled having heard, before leaving Poland, from some Jossele strolling through tavern courtyards. He felt as if he were the teacher in cheder who sought to suggest original images to his pupils, to teach them not only how to write, but how to write poetically, urging them on with incomplete sentences that they had to complete—the Lord will scatter the enemies of Israel as the autumn wind scatters the, the . . . the leaves of the, of the . . . In the same way, he raised the violin on his arm, crossed the instrument with the bow, and then bid the pupil to continue, to vary, to search. The pupil obeyed, evading his gaze. After the lesson the car carried him back home, and once a month the signora's secretary delivered an envelope.

In that era, he had returned to Trieste for a short while, after the war and the extermination. His father never wanted to set foot in Italy again; he never forgave the country for so bitterly disappointing him. Salman remembered the first time his father arrived in Trieste, about a year after the rest of the family. In Poland, in the shtetl where they had lived and where Salman was born, life was not easy for a Jew; certainly, it was much more difficult in the newborn Polish Republic than in the Hapsburg Empire, which had collapsed a few years earlier. He vaguely remembered humiliations, taunts, fears. His father, an orthodox Jew who wore a billowing kaftan and pejes and often spoke Yiddish, had opened a branch office of his firm in Trieste, at the beginning of the thirties, and moved his family there. Italy was Fascist, but it was still not anti-Semitic in that era, especially in Trieste, thanks to the liberal-national and patriotic traditions of the Jewish community. The family quietly became part of the city, and little Salman became a member of a Fascist youth organization. A year later, their father joined them and remained enthusiastic about the family's situation, finally serene. He was particularly proud of his young son's black uniform, a military honor difficult to imagine for a Jewish boy in Poland. Wearing his old kaftan, he used to force little Salman to walk the streets dressed in uniform, and when he saw a Fascist leader, he would say to him, "Hejb die Hand, meschugge! (Raise your hand and salute, idiot!)." Then he would add with satisfaction, "This Mojschale"—so he called Mussolini— "does everything for the Jews."

Afterward Salman's father also moved to Trieste, for love of Mojschale-Mussolini. They all had to flee in the end, because the racial laws were instituted. From that time on, Salman felt that life was, even in other circumstances, the misunderstanding of someone who confuses Mussolini with Mojschale. They traveled from Bilgoray to Trieste, from Trieste to Palestine and America, and then to Trieste again. What had brought him back to that city lost in the course of history, to that last beach of old Europe? Hejb die Hand, meschugge!

He resumed his climb up the road. Before and beneath him lay the sea, an extreme entity, an ultimate opening in front of which he withdrew in atavistic Continental distrust. As a boy, arriving in Trieste and catching his first glimpse of the sea, he had watched the sun set into that blueness, and from that moment the sea, even the small gulf where the Adriatic ended, always remained for him the place where the sun set, the oceanic solitude that those words *Occident* and *West* evoked in him. His central Europe was composed of plains, mountains, houses— places where one was well sheltered, inexpensive hotels where one's face and hands were washed in a basin—and it ended where the water began, any water, any sea. He had even attempted—the only time in his life he had done so—to translate into notes, into the language he understood so well and taught to generations of pupils at the conservatory, that music he heard murmuring like a siren with the sweetest palatal consonants, but he was unable to devise anything. It isn't proper for sirens to sing to a Jew from Bilgoray. Perhaps even his old pupil, whose concerts had enjoyed a certain fame for several years, could have composed something on that summons and that repulse, on that utmost shore, on that desire to divert his gaze from the sea that faced the West and direct it backward, to the familiar, oily East of his ancestors, to that other Europe. But Salman had never spoken to the man about it; he was not so generous as to present him with that agonizing indecision. Besides, for years they never had occasion to speak; when the pupil, in addition to managing his estates, became a violinist who toured half of Europe, it was he who became the Maestro.

Salman arrived at the gate, and at once a servant showed him into the sitting room. Almost nothing had changed; only the signora, the mother, had died, and a person's death scarcely ruffles reality, as Salman knew quite well, he who belonged to a people accustomed to dying by the millions without deviating a millimeter from their path. Vilardi came to meet him with obsequious, condescending affection. In his fattened face, his eyes had become smaller, two sharp, restless slits. He inquired politely about his guest's health, about his family, about how he felt now that he was retired. The conversation continued, cordial and vague, for half an hour. Beyond the veranda, the sea was motionless, the color of iron.

"I would like to show you something, Maestro," Vilardi suddenly said, eagerly leaning forward until nearly brushing against him, with a closeness that to Salman, despite the promiscuously crowded ghetto generations running through his veins, felt unseemly for a moment, almost repulsive. "Playing is beautiful, of course, a unique art, and I, thanks to you, in the end I can say . . . but after so many years, and so many concerts, and so much music by the great ones, and others, I thought that perhaps . . . So the idea crossed my mind—no, the fact is, they asked me—in a word, it seems that for '92 there will be, that they want, for the inauguration, a musical work on Europe, the spirit of united Europe, and besides, for such a long time now I have been thinking about a plan for a composition, and if you would like to take a look at it—naturally, this is only a beginning, a rough draft . . ."

Vilardi quickly turned, opened a drawer, pulled out a sheaf of pages, and offered them to Salman, holding them greedily in his fingers like one of those Jewish peddlers whom Salman remembered from his Polish childhood. "Interesting, interesting," he murmured, taking the pages. He read the opening measures. "A dense language, what's the word—yes, intense—I shall read them attentively, of course, but it is obvious that judging from this opening, it is really . . ." The other man looked at him, his mouth soft and weak beneath rapacious eyes. "And if you could tell me what you think of it or perhaps give me some advice . . . ?" Salman lifted his eyes, still full of the notes he had read on the sheet, and met Vilardi's for a moment; he tried to divert his gaze and at the same time to change his expression, but he realized that the hesitant, contradictory order issued by the cerebral cortex had arrived much too late. Perhaps, like the panting, his diminished quickness was also a distant skirmish. They remained in silence for several seconds; then the master of the house withdrew, dropping into an armchair in a careless, relaxed attitude. "At your leisure, naturally. There's no hurry, and yet, among other things, the director of the theater in Salzburg, just a week ago . . . Above all, I was thinking that you might be interested in a passage further on, as you will see, a passage I have called Kaddish, an homage to the Jewish tragedy, the European tragedy."

"Ah, of course, this, truly . . ." Salman stood up. "Thank you, thank you for your trust. In a few weeks, then . . ."

"Of course, very well, there's no hurry—when I return from New York, from this American *tournée*. Now, if you will allow me, I shall accompany you to the car."

Nearly lying down in the automobile, Salman looked at the objects flying by on either side and felt, after this glance, that the villa and the sitting room and the veranda were now behind him forever. He again saw the other man's eyes reading his and asked himself what purpose was served by the ancestral habit of keeping one's eyelids lowered, if precisely at a certain moment, because of the stupid slowness of one's reflexes, the curtain had to be raised and a look inside irreparably permitted. Some raindrops began to fall, and he closed the window, irritated. Irreparably? He noticed that his pants were unbuttoned in front, as often happened, and he carefully fastened the two buttons. Perhaps it was unnecessary to place a tragic construction on a glance, however painful, and the feeling that something decisive had occurred. His father was dead, the signora was dead, along with many others who had died in much more terrible ways, while he had continued to teach at the conservatory, to eat, to sleep, to lie—at the most, he had increasingly taken it easy. Should an embarrassing glance weigh more heavily than aging, than trust in Mojschale, than dying, should it be some inexplicable revelation? It wasn't a case of being made ridiculous. He would have read the score and, in the end, with interest, although it was as if he were already familiar with it. But in fact there could be, there certainly were, felicitous cues, skillful and pleasant passages, several pardonable gaucheries to be corrected, and some imagination and passion as well. Yes, it was highly probable that he could sincerely praise the composition, and that he would even like it, perhaps he much more than anyone else.

(1990)

Wicked Memories

Barbara Alberti

GRANDMA SANTINA LOVED GOD and hated men. But she didn't hurt anyone. Because not even her brooding, impassioned rancor toward everybody made her forget her fear. After Grandpa's death, no stranger ever entered the house again. His right-hand man stood at the door, gave an account of the errands, and took off like the wind as they slammed the door behind him.

The family had three kinds of enemies. First enemy: the Others.

All the others. They were always on the lookout to snatch away the secrets of the house.

The Others wanted to know what we were cooking, how much money we had, and whether we got along. They

---

Born in Umbria in 1946, BARBARA ALBERTI *lives in Rome. A novelist, playwright, and screenwriter, she has published several novels, only one of which,* Delirium *(1978), has appeared in English. Her irreverent fiction often combines themes of religion, sexuality, and childhood. Her film credits include* The Night Porter *and* The Master and Margherita. *The source of these rural vignettes is her first novel,* Memorie malvage *(Wicked Memories, 1976).*

lived only to get hold of this information, which they'd then use for mysterious plots against us.

You must never talk to the Others. If you were forced to talk, you must never reveal anything.

Grandma called them "the filthy dogs."

Second enemy: the Bolsheviks.

The Bolsheviks were in a distant land full of snow, preparing to attack us. Grandma described them as having huge fur coats and white eyeless masks. Armed with scythes, like Death. They were making an arduous journey through wolves and sleet, singing blasphemies and laughing at the Madonna. And all this just to come and kill us. The children too. And then they'd steal everything.

We prayed a lot against the Bolsheviks. So God might make them sink under ground, straight to Hell.

Grandma called them "filthy dogs" too and made a furtive gesture of spitting in a precise direction, where Russia was, according to her.

And then there was the suspicion that the Others might be Bolsheviks too.

Because those who came from far away had treacherous allies among us.

Whoever didn't go to church, whoever drank, whoever dressed badly could be a Bolshevik.

Third enemy: the Devil.

What a terrible enemy the Devil is!

With the Others and the Bolsheviks all you had to do was close the door, say a rosary, and that was it.

But Satan takes all forms, Satan is the world.

None of his appearances escaped my notice. Satan is the

only one who looks at himself in the mirror without ever saying a prayer and tries to distract souls with the deception of light.

Satan is the red cat who impregnates the tabbies and makes them scream with lust on the roofs.

Satan is the moon that rises behind the poplar trees and parodies the consecrated host.

Satan is the music that comes from the street and makes you laugh for no reason.

Satan is everywhere, and the ribbon salesman is his slave when he goes knocking from door to door to tempt virtuous wives. (The Others were steady customers of the salesman and, in a broad sense, of Satan himself.)

Satan is inside the mirror. All you have to do is look into your eyes. And then immediately you must cross yourself, without losing a moment, and turn away from your image.

Only once I wasn't shrewd enough, and I barely got away in time—already a slender horn was coming out of the mirror, waving to and fro.

Satan is the sea, sky, night, and day, Satan is the cripple who panhandles to buy a drink.

Satan is the poor man who has no patience.

Satan is in church in the girls' red lips. Satan is at the movie theater, in the first row, when no one is permitted to see the movie. His presence summons the sinners like a burning magnet, and the Prince of Darkness sneers in the dark.

I used to know all the Demon's tricks. When I was by myself, and it was so quiet he seemed to be gone, I would hear his mute breathing, muffled by the clock.

In the corners of the house, behind the bookcase, you could see the sharp point of his tail.

I ran to turn on the light when I heard him above me, ready to snatch me, but he was diabolically quick and hid again.

There were only two ways to fight him. The electric light and the sign of the cross.

Yet at night, if the Devil managed to enter your sleep, look out. He laughed at the sign of the cross, he laughed at the light. He was as careful during the day as he was impudent in dreams, where he appeared with his red goat's face, and I was the only one who saw him.

I made desperate signs to Grandma, who didn't understand and squeezed me, and it seemed she held me tight so he could torment me more.

I begged her to pray, and she sang. I began to suspect that she might be in cahoots with him.

And from the way she shook her head, from the way her nails grew sharp in my dreams, I suddenly understood one night that it was all a very ugly deception.

Grandma Santina and the Devil were the same person.

After years of sins, after countless girls had shown their legs in church, after the cows were struck with pestilence (only a warning), the Evil One manifested his presence in Gelsomino's bakery one day, a little after noon.

The shop boy had red hair, which was already a bad sign, and he was a lazy, impure orphan. He threw himself to the ground shouting and slobbering all over.

The priest and the people ran to see the possessed boy. The children were taken back home and Gigi Ridolfi hit his wife, Palmina, who always wore a little too much makeup.

The priest and Gelsomino, shut in the shop with the

boy, tried to cast out the Devil, who tempted them in a woman's voice.

But the struggle against him is hard. The doctor entered the shop with an authoritative air, as if the matter were his concern.

He cleaned the boy's head and said he was an epileptic. Then he carried him away and gave him some medicine instead of the prayers that would have cured him.

The truth came out despite the medicine, despite the unbelieving doctor's tricks.

Satan loves to show himself.

A little while later, just outside the bakery, the boy fell down shouting, a green dribble running from his gaping mouth. He beat his head against the ground and tore at his clothes.

Gelsomino closed the shop and the people watched the Demon's power without making a move.

The boy was full of blood. The priest was more prudent this time. He sprinkled the boy with holy water, keeping a few steps away from him, until a jet of fire and sulphur issued from the sinner's mouth, marking Gelsomino's door. Gelsomino came outside on his knees confessing his sin with the boy, begging forgiveness from God and the people who stared straight at him, maliciously, without batting an eye.

There are no photographs of that incident. Only Grandma Santina's stories and her fear of such an unnatural and atrocious sin.

Gelsomino continued to live in a roach-infested room, sunk in his excrement and in the obscene words that the children shouted at him from beneath the windows.

The boy died soon after. The Demon took him in hand and they found him with his head split open, which he himself had struck against the ground.

No one could know how many dark doors there might be in Grandma Santina's Tower, doors that closed one after another in a labyrinth of sorrow.

But it was known that one of them was always locked.

At the back of the storeroom for wood, where you never had to go. If I'd only gone near it, an animal with a spider's head, as big as two cows, would've jumped out and eaten me. It loved the taste of children; I didn't go there.

I was good, obedient, and in God's grace.

Grandma used to go there with bowls of soup and, sometimes, in the silence of prayer, the sound of weeping came from the closed room. Everyone said, "Listen to the frogs, in the stream."

But the frogs wept with a man's voice.

An autumn of green mists came. Almost everyone forgot the blue of the sky. The people in the village quickly got used to it; they didn't ask why and waited for winter.

I felt that God's grace had abandoned me, and I continually thought about the closed door.

The Devil exploited this weakness and created an occasion of sin. One afternoon Grandma Santina, driven by the ringing bells to run to church, left the keys to all the doors on the kitchen table.

I was alone.

I stared at the keys and murmured, "Sweet heart of Mary, be my soul's deliverance."

A cat jumped up onto the table and his meowing was joined by that soft weeping, always the same, coming from the closed door.

"O Jesus who suffered on the cross, make me listen to your voice."

Silence.

I took the keys.

A wake of darkness followed my remorseful, damned steps toward the wood store.

The key was huge.

I turned it several times in the lock and shut my eyes so I couldn't see the monster who'd eat me.

But the monster wasn't there.

On a bed without a sheet lay an old, hairy man, who seemed to be crying, and he laughed, his eyes sunken beneath his eyebrows.

His laughter was reassuring; it clearly showed that he had no teeth so he couldn't eat children.

He made a sign for me to draw near, and with a contented air he showed me something that he secretively held tight in his hand, as if he were afraid it'd be stolen from him.

It was a little tail, white as a stone, which stuck out between his legs.

I then understood why they kept him locked up. He was a relative with a tail, and that oddity must've made Grandma Santina ashamed. The old man took my hand to make me touch the tail, which was soft; my fingers sank into it, and it had hair all around but not on top (just the opposite of animals' tails).

I played a little while with the tail, which got stronger bit by bit with a pleasantness that wasn't at all like Hell, while night gradually fell and only his eyes and the tail stood out among the shadowed things.

The authoritative ringing of the bells broke off that game, just when some milk, thick and white like a snail's track, began to come out of the tail. Running quickly I closed the door again and placed the keys on the kitchen table, exactly where Grandma had left them.

And when she came with her veil on her head and her rosary cross dangling outside her pocket, I stroked the cat's tail in the hope that it might stand up a little, like the man's. But in spite of my caresses, the tail stayed the same, and I made silent comparisons, all at the cat's expense, while I pleasantly hummed:

> Sweet heart of Jesus,
> make me love you more and more;
> sweet heart of Mary,
> be my soul's deliverance.

One Good Friday, after supper, Grandma Santina furtively started toward the locked room with a bowl of soup.

Everyone pretended they didn't see her go down the stairs and head toward the wood store.

When the key turned with the racket of rusty chains, they raised their voices to muffle the noise.

And everything was absorbed in the silence of the Tower, in the fiction that nothing happened outside of the good Lord's laws.

But suddenly we heard a terrible noise, so terrible that no one dared to go on talking, and an old but determined voice shouted with more than a thousand echoes, "Damn it! Give me a piece of ass!"

Even our breathing was paralyzed in the huge kitchen.

Running with her eyes wide open and one hand on her soup-stained face, my dishevelled Grandma rushed in front of the stove and knelt down sobbing before the Madonna on the calendar.

And before anyone could even think of what to do, the locked-up old man, my secret friend, burst into the kitchen with his pants unbuttoned and his white tail almost upright and decisively shouted to Grandma, who was moaning all kinds of prayers, "I want a cunt, right this minute!"

The maid laughed. Uncle Leo and the hired laborer jumped on the old man, who struggled and continued to shout his demand.

Instead of what he asked for, he got a punch in the mouth from the laborer.

They dragged him back to his room, and from then on you didn't hear his frogs' weeping, his laughter that seemed like weeping.

Later, and only by accident, I knew that they'd silenced him until his death, which God delayed only so Grandma might earn a good spot in heaven.

The men of death rushed in.

Dressed in black, with tape measures in their hands and a tearful manner.

Finally they opened the locked door in front of everyone.

The old man with the tail had ended his imprisonment. He left the room only to get into a coffin, and they quickly forgot about him. Lazzaro Baldassari, 92, died on March 26th.

An honest worker, he'd emigrated to Australia, where

he'd earned and saved, bringing honor to the name of his native land.

He returned already old, with a little money and the beginnings of arteriosclerosis.

In a short time he forgot what he had experienced.

He forgot the journeys and the labor.

He forgot fear and good deeds.

For the rest of his days he remembered only sex, which he'd denied and neglected, and now in the confusion of actions which were blurred, it seemed to him the only thing worthy of attention.

Because of this they kept him locked up, pretending he didn't exist. A muffled sigh of relief accompanied his death.

His room became a storeroom for flour.

Covered with holy pictures that were pinned to his jacket, the distributor of Madonnas passed through once a month.

Gerolamo di San Sebastiano, vendor of cruel sorrows, went singing through the village. During his walk he used to trail an iron chain.

He had red eyes and white eyebrows, and to escape the curse that afflicts albinos marked by God, he'd devoted himself to the holy trade.

His journey was not affected by wind and mountains. His home was the path of the pilgrim.

His shrine, a northern printing house where the Madonnas he designed himself, in a frenzy of salvation, were printed for him.

At the home of Grandma Santina he was a guest of

honor. They gave him two-pound steaks to make up for his fasts, and he drained liters of wine to recover his strength after penance.

He had the face of a wicked animal.

They treated him like a saint.

He ate with his hands, and the chain, which he never removed, clinked at each mouthful.

At the end of the meal he belched and disguised this excess with a cry of thanksgiving to heaven.

His Madonnas had gaping mouths and sky-blue gowns. On the back was the stamp of the diocese which blessed them, for a commission.

Even if Gerolamo denied having any superhuman power, the fame of his miracles spread through the entire region.

When the crop ran the risk of going bad, when the rain was late, from afar one heard Gerolamo's song, and the women wept contented. It was enough to buy a Madonna from him, to ask him to remember you in his prayers, and misfortunes were averted.

Of course. Even if his modesty stopped him from admitting it, Gerolamo did not invent the images of the Madonna.

It was known that the Blessed Virgin appeared to him on top of a mountain, and that the distributor of the Madonnas did portraits from life.

So powerful were Heaven's favors that even cases of sterility were resolved through Gerolamo.

Many unfortunate wives turned their prayers to him, and some time afterward their homes were blessed with children.

Olga nel Norcino told me that my mother had been

among the first to have the miracle. She was young and in despair, and the doctors refused to believe that she could have a child.

But she had faith.

My mother had to remain shut in a room with Gerolamo only once for the holy rites, and her marriage was made joyful and perhaps saved by my birth.

The great flood came in silence.

The streets turned into rivers.

Trees and houses were overturned in the water.

Everything was covered. Because of the rooms closed in sin, because of the lies and the thefts, because of stinginess toward God.

Satan triumphed gurgling in the mud.

The drowned surfaced with sad faces.

Marione's paralytic daughter crossed the village on the chair where they'd tied her in order to save her. As the chair rocked, she shook her head, as if she were alive.

From the top of the Tower, Grandma Santina watched the people who escaped fate on boats full of belongings and corpses. The rain made her white as an old fish. Uncle Leo had offered to take her away with the cats. But she had resisted her diabolical ambition to imitate Noah.

And she knew that the elect would be saved.

God's lesson lasted thirty days.

The water came up to Grandma's knees, as she stood on the roof. Many died. Many were left to die. The deluge was near.

(1976)

A Geographical Error

Romano Bilenchi

THE INHABITANTS of the city of F. don't know geography, the geography of their country, of their own home. When I left G. to study at F., I immediately noticed that these people had a mistaken idea of the location of my native town. As soon as I mentioned G., they told me, "Oh, you're from the Maremma."

One day, then, while the professor of Italian was explaining the work of some ancient Italian writer I no longer recall, he began to speak of certain shepherds who in the windows of their huts hung sheepskin tanned very finely instead of glass. For some reason I stood up from the last desk, where I was sitting, and said, "Yes, it's true: among us as well farm workers attach the skins of rabbits or sheep to

---

A journalist as well as a novelist, ROMANO BILENCHI *(1909–1989) was born in Colle di Val d'Elsa, a town that lies between Florence and Siena. During World War II he participated in the resistance and joined the Italian Communist Party, from which he resigned in 1957 after the repression of riots in Poland. This piece is drawn from* Anna and Bruno *(1938), a short-story collection that addresses themes of childhood and adolescence.*

---

their cabin windows in place of glass, so great is their poverty." For some reason I stood up and said this. Perhaps I wanted to make myself seem clever to the professor; perhaps I was driven by a humanitarian impulse on behalf of poor people and I wanted to testify to my classmates, all of them city dwellers, that the professor had said something right, that such poverty really existed in the world. Apart from the poverty, however, the affirmation was a product of my imagination. In my life—God knows whether I had ever wandered around the countryside—only once did I happen to see a windowpane patched with a piece of paper; and the farmer's wife, moreover, had practically apologized, saying that as soon as someone from the family could go to the city, they would buy a brand new window pane. No sooner was I standing before the class than I felt every impulse checked, and I realized that I had said something very stupid. I hoped that the professor might not be familiar with the customs of my region, but at my outburst, he raised his head from his book and said, "Don't talk nonsense." After a moment, he laughed and everybody followed suit, if only to please him. "But wait a minute," he then said. "Perhaps you're right. Your town, G., isn't it in the Maremma? In the Maremma they probably still dress in sheepskin."

Everybody burst into laughter again. Someone, perhaps to point out that the professor and I were on the same level of stupidity, guffawed ambiguously. I turned to grasp that uncertain yet unique solidarity with my position, but the first classmate I encountered, to avoid compromising himself, called me "Bagpiper" and imitated playing the bagpipes characteristic of rural areas. Another said, "Did you ever see sheep dung?" and in a chorus the others chanted, "Baa, baa!"

I began—this was my error—to respond to each of them as they opened their mouths. I was one of the smallest and most ingenuous students in the class, and very soon the whole gang preyed upon me. Although they belonged to distinguished families, the class included the son of a nouveau riche shopkeeper, as I gathered from the mammas and daddies who would come to the school every month: they spoke their minds to me. Finally, with tears in my eyes, taking advantage of a moment of silence, I shouted, "Professor, G. is not in the Maremma."

"It is in the Maremma."

"No, it is not in the Maremma."

"It *is* in the Maremma," said the professor resolutely. "I have friends all across your region and often I go to hunt larks with them. I know the town well. It is in the Maremma."

"We natives of G. also go to hunt larks in the Maremma. But the Maremma is at least eighty kilometers from my town. We see it as a very different place. Besides, G. is a city," I said.

"But I've seen herdsmen precisely at the market in G.," he responded.

"That's impossible. I've always lived there and I've never seen any herdsmen."

"Don't insist. You wouldn't be trying to suggest that I'm an idiot, would you?"

"I'm not trying to do anything," I said. "But G. is not in

the Maremma. Traveling peddlers come to the market dressed as redskins. Because of this you could assert that G. is in America."

"You're also witty," he said. "But before calling you stupid and throwing you out of the class, I shall demonstrate to your classmates that G. is located in the Maremma." He sent a boy to fetch the map of the region from the science classroom, so that there too they knew about my dispute and were amusing themselves at my expense. On the map, despite the fact that I didn't allow a single one of his assertions to go unchallenged, the professor abolished the actual boundaries of the province, created new imaginary ones, and managed to convince my classmates, relying on the scale of 1:1,000,000, along with various other fabrications, that G. is really in the Maremma.

"It isn't true that G. is in the Maremma," I finally struck back, "since we take 'Maremmano' to be synonymous with an uncouth, ignorant man."

"In you, then," he concluded, "we have the proof that the people of G. are authentic Maremmani. I have known few boys as uncouth and ignorant as you. You're still wearing those shaggy knee socks." At that point, he looked me up and down. The others did the same. I felt I wasn't as elegant as my classmates. I fell silent, humiliated. From that day onward I was the "Maremmano." But what irritated me most, in the end, was the geographical ignorance of the professor and my classmates.

I could not bear the Maremma. I had been seized by an intense aversion at the first document that happened to come before my eyes concerning the territory and its inhabitants. I had previously read many books about the horsemen of the American prairies, and I had seen innumerable films about their astounding adventures—books and films that had excited me. A couple years of my life had been dedicated to the horses, lassoes, huge hats, and pistols of those extraordinary men. In my heart there was no room for anybody else. When they arrived to free sidekicks captured by the Indians, I felt that their fluttering little flag represented freedom; and I would have hurled myself at the throat of whoever declared himself on the side of White Deer and Son of Eagle. When the wagon train, forced to form a circle to brave the attack of the murderous Indians, would return joyful and ready to set forth over the immense deserted prairies and the deep mountain gorges, I felt as if men had again won the right to traverse the world. The names of those horsemen—I used to know the names of every hero of every serialized novel and every film—were always on my lips. I judged every person by comparing him to them, and very few withstood the comparison. When I read that a stone's throw from my house—one might say—there lived men who lassoed wild animals, tamed bulls, dressed in Far West gear (more or less), and camped at night beneath the starry sky wrapped in blankets around blazing fires with their rifles and faithful dogs close by, I burst into a fit of laughter. I couldn't even take seriously the stories about the faithful dogs, which are common and accepted throughout the world. I poured over many maps and increasingly convinced myself that in an area so close to me there couldn't possibly be wild animals, brave men, or any likelihood of adventures. Nor could there be the sweetest dark-haired women who sang on canvas-covered wagons and, if need be, loaded their partners' weapons. No, the horsemen of the Maremma were poor copies of the heroes of my acquaintance. Those in the books and films constantly fought against Indians and robbers; but there, a stone's throw away, what robbers could there be? The era of the famous old bandits seemed to be distant, if they had ever existed; I had my doubts about them as well.

When I went to study at F., this is precisely the way I thought. I could not therefore stand the nickname "Maremmano."

I used to play football with skill, but also with a certain roughness, notwithstanding that I was small and thin. I immediately distinguished myself the first time I went on the field with my classmates, and they put me at inside left forward on the squad that represented the secondary school in the student championship. I played several games, earning much applause.

"The Maremmano is good," they would say. "He must've been trained with the wild colts. The herdsmen taught him a bunch of sly tricks."

The gibes and taunts, since I was certain that they contained some sincere praise, did not in fact irritate me. I would smile and the others quickly fell silent. We were now close to the end of the championship with a good chance of coming in first, and I promised myself that, because of services rendered in the school's honor—imagine a game won by a single point that I had scored—I would not be called "Maremmano" in future. In the last match, however, an ugly incident occurred. On the way downfield I happened to turn my back to the opposing goal. They passed me the ball from the right. I turned to shoot on the volley. The goalie had guessed the move and dove forward to block both leg and ball, but my kick caught him squarely in the mouth. He passed out. I had broken three of his teeth. His mates heaped threats on me. I said that I hadn't done it on purpose, it was an accident, I was a close friend of the goalie, who was staying in the very same pensione as me, but the students supporting the other squad, who were very numerous in the audience, began to shout, "Maremmano, Maremmano, Maremmano."

I saw red, and turning toward the spectators who were shouting more loudly, I made an obscene gesture. The referee sent me off the field. As I was leaving, the shouts and insults intensified. I saw that even the girls were shouting.

"Maremmano, Maremmano, Maremmano—he comes from G."

My teammates must have been among those who were shouting. How else could everyone know that I was born in G.? I felt deprived of any solidarity and, head lowered, I walked toward the dressing room.

"Maremmano, Maremmano, Maremmano, you're still wearing those shaggy knee socks."

The fact that the others didn't like my knee socks was unimportant to me. It was a question of taste. I have always liked woolen things, handmade and rather heavy. To me the socks were very handsome, and I didn't blame them for my troubles, even though they were constantly the object of critical remarks and satire. On that occasion too, I was angered above all by the injustice my tormentors were committing against G. by continuing to believe that it was located in the Maremma. I went back to the spectators and sought to explain the error that those ignorant people were making, but by dint of the laughter, shouts, pushes, and even kicks in the pants, I was chased to the dressing room.

The next day the headmaster summoned me and suspended me for a week because of the gesture I had made to the spectators, a gesture that dishonored the school. I opened my heart to the headmaster, hoping that at least he might understand that G. was not in the Maremma. He listened to me at length, but his face wore the same derisive expression as my classmates', and at the end of my speech, he confirmed the punishment. Perhaps he believed that I was something of an idiot.

My first impulse was to write home and beg my father and mother to send me to study in another city. But how could I explain my punishment? I would not have been understood; in fact, they would have scolded me. They were making sacrifices to support me at school. I decided to put up with everything. On my return to school after the suspension, the offenses against G. and me multiplied. Summer was approaching, however, and with summer, vacation would come. At home I would think about what to do the following year; perhaps I would abandon my studies and find a job. But just then the worst trouble befell me.

One Sunday morning, having left my pensione early to enjoy the bright colors of late spring, I saw the walls plastered with vivid posters and groups of people lingering to admire them. The three figures that stood out in the posters immediately made me turn up my nose: a bull, his head lowered as if in the act of hurling himself into the street; a slender colt pawing the ground; and a herdsman who was looking at the two animals with contemptuous self-confidence. I drew closer. The posters announced that next Sunday, in a field near the hippodrome, for the first time in a city, the horsemen of the Maremma would perform in thrilling feats of derring-do.

I had never been in the Maremma, nor had I ever seen the herdsmen except in photographs. A better occasion to laugh at them could not have been offered to me. Besides, I liked immensely the place where the event would take place. As the river leaves the city, it withdraws into the countryside through bizarre bends, finally free of the houses and bridges. Between the right riverbank and a row of hills lie some very beautiful parks with wooden cafés and enormous trees; there are also pretty green meadows surrounded by well-kept boxwood hedges, which suddenly open up amid the trees. I liked the green meadows and hedges even more than the riverbank, and on the afternoons when I did not have class, I would never miss going to visit them. I would sit at the borders, next to the hedges, and from there observe the low, tender grass, which filled my soul with joy.

"I shall go there Sunday," I decided, and at noon, on my return to the pensione, I invited my messmates, the goalie I had injured in the football match, and two students in my secondary school to go to the performance with me.

"We've already seen the posters," said the goalie. "We'll come to admire your teachers." The others also accepted and on the appointed day we walked to the site of the performance. I was not expecting the huge crowd, drawn there, I thought, more by the splendid day than by the herdsmen and their animals. There were beautiful ladies and girls, just like at the races. I had already begun looking at the women who went strolling near the hippodrome on Sundays. Following the crowd we entered a field, where on one side several stands had been constructed. I suddenly realized that I was no longer with my mates; perhaps the throng had separated us. I found a place to sit.

A wild colt entered the arena, along with a few herdsmen dressed in the style of cowboys from overseas. I was immediately annoyed by their clothing. The colt started to wander confusedly through the field. A herdsman rushed up behind it. His task was to mount the horse from behind on the run and to remain mounted despite the animal's fits of rage. But the colt, having noticed the man, stopped and allowed him to approach. Then the herdsman, perhaps unsettled by the presence of so many people, made a leap and wound up nearly astride the colt's neck. It was the way to mount a wooden horse, and yet horse and rider fell to the earth. The other herdsmen ran to help. The colt didn't want to stand up; it held the man prisoner, pressing its belly on his legs. The audience began to shout. The colt eventually decided to get on its feet again and, very calmly, allowed itself to be led out of the field.

"He won't be tamed," shouted a spectator. "He's a lamb."

The crowd erupted into noisy laughter. I too laughed with relish.

A bull entered the green clearing. A herdsman confronted it at once, trying to grasp it by the horns and bring it down. The audience was hushed. The bull seemed more alert than the colt. In fact, the roles were quickly reversed—it seemed as if the bull had been assigned the task of knocking down the man. The animal began to behave with a kind of strange craftiness: it enacted a long series of feints like a football player who wants to pass an opponent. It finally charged the man, driving him to take to his heels. Yet it was a charge full of caution, without hostility, as if the bull had wanted to mock the enemy's gruff attitude, and the spectators immediately realized that the herdsman had not suffered any harm. Once again the other herdsmen ran to help their mate. Then the bull began running merrily after those poor devils. It headed for the hedges and, after completing two laps around the field, dashed in the direction of the river. The herdsmen, now in despair, also vanished beyond the hedge amid the uproar of the audience.

The crowd was yelling and cursing. In the end, aware that there would be no other attractions, they began to disperse.

"Swindlers," they shouted.

"It's a scandal."

"What robbery!"

"Down with the Maremmani!"

"We want our money back."

I shouted along with the others. Someone landed several blows on the booth where the tickets for the stands had been sold. I threw a stone at the wooden tables: I wanted to see everything destroyed. At the exit my mates surrounded me.

"We were looking for you," said one.

"You were hiding, weren't you?"

"Your paisans were just great. All of you should reimburse the spectators for the price of the ticket."

"He too is a Maremmano," said the goalie, pointing me out to people nearby.

"He's a Maremmano, just like these swindlers who jerked us around."

A crowd of boys gathered and started to ridicule me as if they had always known me.

"Don't you think he's a Maremmano?" said the goalie again. "Look at his knee socks. That's the kind of stuff they wear in Maremma."

"Tomorrow I'll wear cotton socks," I said. "I wear them every year when it gets warm." Then I added, "G. is not in the Maremma."

At the mention of G. several adults made common cause with the boys.

"Tell your countrymen they're thieves," said a young man. The others laughed. With tears in my eyes I then tried to explain the grave error they committed by thinking that G. was located in the Maremma.

"Is he a bit touched?" someone asked one of my mates.

"More than a bit," he replied.

The boys were shouting more loudly than before. They started pushing me, the adults no less than the boys.

A young man ran up; he was laughing and said that he had been to the river. The bull had thrown himself into the water, and the herdsmen were weeping, cursing, and begging the saints and the bull, but they were unable to drag him out. At this news the attacks on me intensified.

"He must be the son of the herdsmen's boss if he defends them so much," said a girl.

"No," I hollered. "I'm not defending them. I hate them. I have nothing to do with them. My grandfather owned farms. My mother is a lady. It was she who made these socks."

"They're made of goat hair," said an old gentleman. One boy emitted a "Baa," another a "Moo," and a third gave me a punch.

I turned around. I was standing in the middle of a street that leads to the city. People were gathering behind me in a semicircle. I was crying. It must have been a long time since I had cried. I broke away from the group and leaned against a tree. Far away, on the shore of the river, I glimpsed my mates running in the opposite direction. Perhaps they were going to see the bull who had thrown himself in the river.

(1938)

A Bender

Federigo Tozzi

NOW THAT I'VE TURNED FORTY, I feel like tak-
ing a wife. Fact is, I've thought quite a lot about marrying,
but I've never really made up my mind. I work at the railroad, was stationmaster for a long while. I began my career
in a little village in the Marches, then was sent to Tuscany,
then just outside of Bologna, and now I'm in Florence.

Tonight I'm going to write to the woman who was my
landlady in Tuscany and ask her if she's willing to marry
me. I'm doing this after being here for six years; and I can't
really explain why. Fact is, it hadn't ever dawned on me.

She's a widow, on a pension from the railroad; and I
believe she doesn't find me disagreeable. She isn't a knock-
out: she's portly, her teeth are gappy and decayed, her nose
seems swollen. But her house was always very clean; and
she was always very kind to me. From her kitchen window

FEDERIGO TOZZI *(1883–1920) was born in Siena. He worked
briefly for the state railroad and later managed farms, experiences that
provided material for his unsettling novels and stories. Tozzi's forte
was the realistic narrative that scrutinizes the lives of alienated, dis-
illusioned characters. Recent translations include the novel* Eyes Shut
(1990) and the collection of stories Love in Vain *(2001).*

you could see mine, since both opened onto a narrow plastered courtyard. A few cats were usually there, meowing, looking up. The other windows, all small ones, stood before a table with a row of potted flowers, almost all geraniums. We used to hang the washing out to dry. Signora Costanza—this is the name of the woman I'd like to marry—did lots of washing, and very often I'd waste time standing at the window to watch her stockings and blouses dangling. The stockings were all red, the blouses a heavy cloth with pointy lace around the collar. When she used to look out from the kitchen and spot me, I'd blush.

But maybe now I understand why I never thought about courting her. This has happened to me before: I'd fall in love after a while, when I'd stopped living near a particular place. But this time I'm really giving it some thought; and I'm amazed I haven't said a word. When I'd come back to the house, I used to find her reading, if it wasn't already dark. For years and years she'd always be reading the same book—*The Three Musketeers*. Some pages were yellow with grease, but the book had been covered in newspaper. When she'd see me, she'd set it down and pet the cat that was sitting on her knee.

"Buona sera!"

"Welcome home. Are you tired?"

"Bushed."

"Do you want to light the lamp?"

"Thanks; I've got matches."

I'd rummage throught my pocket, pull out a wooden match and strike it on the floor because the wall would've been cleaned when I was gone. I'd find the oil lamp in the room. Ah, I was always thinking about the electric light at the station! I'd change my jacket, wash my hands; then I'd go into the parlor to eat. Signora Costanza, always punctual, would've already set the table; fact is, sometimes she'd be waiting for me to take a seat. The cat had already curled up between our two chairs. Then she'd begin. When I'd eat at the trattoria to save time, I always thought of that parlor; and Signora Costanza felt so lonesome that, if there'd been no gossip, she'd come to see me at the station before I finished my shift.

But we'd never say anything to each other; I don't even think I was her friend. I think that, at least in the beginning, she didn't entirely trust me and was even disappointed. I'd often see her sad, and she looked as if she was growing old; but I never thought of encouraging that half-smile of hers, which I believe was due more to melancholy than being hard up or sick. In the middle of the parlor stood a small oval table covered with an embroidered square of wool, fringed in red and green, and on it sat a bell jar that contained a stuffed sparrow. Two curtains had nearly turned yellow. Fact is—to go back over something I've already mentioned—Signora Costanza had a real liking for animals; she even had a pigeon that was so nice and nimble he'd leap on her bed every morning and give her a peck on the mouth. That pigeon used to follow her all through the house. She'd pick him up and pet him: he'd tremble in her hands and look around with the sweetest eyes, although whether at her or the room I couldn't tell. She also had a cockerel whose wings refused to grow. He slept between the cat's legs and always used to cheep when we'd go and eat.

Sometimes, as I read the newspaper, I'd smoke nearly all

my cigar without getting up from the table. While Signora Costanza was clearing away, she'd ask me, "Is it true a girl was killed with fifteen knife wounds? Has the war really broken out again?"

But if the pigeon leaped onto her shoulder, then she'd start speaking to him. It gave me a strange feeling that I couldn't explain. And I was so accustomed to these things that when they stopped, I had the sense that something bad was going to happen, even though I'm not a superstitious type.

For some ridiculous reason, I went to find the letters and illustrated postcards she'd sent me. Her letters are such a perfect reminder of her that I don't need to read them. I vaguely remember what she wrote in each one, and now they kindle a feeling that resembles comfort. Yes, there she goes, lifting her green glass goblet, like a chalice, the flask of wine, the apple peels, and that slow chewing she recommended to me, as an example, because of my bad digestion.

Now I'm sure she always loved me. How obvious it is! Why else didn't she ever ask me to leave? Why did she tell me she wouldn't have taken on any other boarder? But no, on the other hand, I feel it's impossible; it can't be true. What will they think of it in her village? Won't the coworkers I left behind always be there? No, it's too late now; it'd be useless for me to write to her.

Yet the five years I spent with her are unforgettable; and at some point I'll visit her again. What if she's died? What if she got sick? How much dust would've collected on the bell jar, with the straw stuffing peeking out of that sparrow, its claws clasping the forked twig on the round black pedestal! Did the pigeon die of hunger? Did the cat go down to the courtyard? In the beginning too that parlor filled me with a lingering feeling of sadness: there was something gloomy about it, even frightening, and with the curtains the light seemed mournful. I'd immediately open the windows to let in some air; but nevertheless the parlor always remained the same. I'd never been there without worrying, even when I heard Signora Costanza in the other rooms. Still, sometimes I experienced a sense of peace; I felt like falling asleep there.

When I made my monthly payment, we'd go into the parlor; and paying so punctually always made me feel proud, as if I really enjoyed it. Afterward I used to whistle, and I was happy.

But why would Signora Costanza go there and cry sometimes? The pages of *The Three Musketeers* wet with tears! Even D'Artagnan's face might've been moved—she gave just that impression. And I never asked her why she was so mournful! I was satisfied with the explanation that everyone had vied to give me: she couldn't get over her poor husband.

Rather, those tears would make me think that I too was aging quickly, and I'd soon be dead. Then up through my arms I'd experience a sensation that felt like the sparks made by the telegraph during a storm. All I found was my red cap, even if it was greasy, with the three gold stripes that bore witness to my good service; I didn't forget about all these things! I'd open the drawer and look through my papers, then pick up the photos of my brother and sister; in those days I felt as if they'd lived so much, with an intensity that filled me with envy, almost hatred. It hadn't ever been possible for me: next to them, I was nothing but an extra. But I loved them, loved them so deeply that I felt my heart beat stronger. And then I'd feel like crying. Yet when I thought that Signora Costanza had done the same thing for a dead man, I decided that I shouldn't cry so as not to bring some misfortune on myself. I imagined that I was Signora Costanza's bad luck. But I couldn't smile; I was left with a vague, confused depression; and then I'd feel like returning to work immediately. I'd grab my cap and leave. The village, Poggibonsi, was very noisy at night; the cafés would be filling up. The stream that passed beneath the bridge near the station roared over the stones. Girls walking arm in arm brushed against me with their elbows; guys bumped into me. Someone might call me from a wine shop to have a drink. I'd answer with a smile or, depending on the situation, I'd remove my cap and feel a slight shiver when some ladies were present. Halfway down the street I'd see the kitchen window where Signora Costanza would certainly be sitting, and in those days I'd turn back. But when I thought of her, I sometimes played a joke on myself: I'd imagine that her thin, bony face had turned puffy and swollen. Oh, no, I'd be too tired to return to work; my head was swimming! What would I do if the guy who worked the shift with me was there? I'd left everything perfectly in order; nothing had happened. And the inspector had given me his hand, sensing that I was tipsy in the sight of my subordinates, who I'd treat to frowns, irritably, as if the skin around my eyes had contracted on its own.

Then I'd stroll down the most deserted streets, where you'd hear only women conversing or a gang of boys yelling. A barrel organ would always be playing in an osteria, whose red lamp expected regulars. Passing by it, you'd hear a jumble of curses nearly blending with that cheerful, shrill sound—it seemed like some yokel's laughter. I walked out of the village a bit, meeting farm workers who were returning with their oxen. Or some woman in a window, some silent man smoking in the doorway of a house. The fields, which were much higher than the road constructed between two lateral walls, were covered in shadow; dogs barked, the noise of people faded. I went back. I entered my house and hoped that Signora Costanza might've gone to bed. But she was there, in the parlor, reading the *Book of Dreams,* while *The Three Musketeers* lay closed in the center of the table with a knitting needle inserted to mark the pages she'd read.

I went past, pretending that I didn't want to disturb her; she raised her head, as if to invite me to sit, but didn't dare. I experienced a cruel pleasure in seeing her make that gesture; and in those days, even if I had felt like conversing, I wouldn't have stopped. I took more satisfaction in treating her that way. Before falling asleep, I'd imagine that her reading bothered me, and, yes, because she didn't even whisper! But it didn't matter; it was just an excuse to smother any feeling of friendship, which was now undeniable. Between me and her something had been born, even if it didn't go past that first day.

Sometimes I'd feel like mocking her for keeping all those animals in the house; and I supposed she loved me as much as them. Then I'd look at her in anger.

"What will you have this morning, Signor Vincenzo?"

I'd realize I was wrong. I became more agreeable and smiled at her.

But finally, in short, why did I come to the decision to

marry her? And what will she think of me? Now she'll
believe that everything I said to her was the beginning of
my love, and I don't like that. I bet she'll remember me quite
well—and think I'm trying to play a joke on her. What can
I do to make her believe it immediately? No, I can't trust
anybody else; I've got to go myself. It's better than writing:
I bet some postal worker would open the letter! A letter for
Signora Costanza! But we'll be happy; I'm certain. My
God, why didn't I think of it sooner? The pigeon: will he
be old now? And the cat? All of them here, in this house;
in my house. If we have children, we'll love each other even
more. I'll have our portrait done and send it to my brothers. Oh, how much I'll love her! All the love I never had.
How moved I'll be when I ask her, "Signora Costanza, will
you be my wife?" And she'll respond . . . How will she
respond? I can't imagine. But we'll be so happy together!
Yes, I'll be moved when I tell her, "I couldn't come back
without seeing this house again!" And she'll burst into tears;
I bet she'll just burst into tears. I'll make her cry.

Costanza had died; but her relatives left the parlor intact.
The pigeon had a gammy leg; I saw him.
    Before getting back on the train, I went with my friends,
who took me to have a drink. And since I was too ashamed
to tell them why I'd returned—fact is, I led them to believe
I'd returned just to see them again—they made me get dead
drunk, just to give me a hearty welcome. It was a bender
that became proverbial. I didn't know what I was doing: it
was the first time, and I guzzled the wine by the liter.

(1920)

Voices Borne by Something, Impossible to Say What

Antonio Tabucchi

SOMETIMES IT MIGHT START with a game, nothing
very grand, a child's secret, you alone are familiar with it
but you're too embarrassed ever to tell anyone—these
things just aren't done—still it's a game, or let's call it a joke
you play on yourself, or on other people, occasional
passersby, the odd bystander, even if they don't know your
game, they're the unwitting players. Because they speak.
The game's simple, costs nothing, lacks any rules unless
you yourself set them, this makes it attractive and easy, and
all you need do is to wander around, on a Sunday, for
instance, Sunday's an ideal day with all the couples moving bored through cafés, the gangs of old friends telling
stories to one another, the loners buttonholing waiters, lit-

ANTONIO TABUCCHI, *born in Pisa in 1943, lives in
Florence. A specialist in Portuguese literature, he has translated the
work of Fernando Pessoa. Tabucchi's fiction incisively explores the
relations between psychology, identity, and action; recently he has
turned to social and political issues. Most of his novels and story
collections are available in English, including* Pereira Declares
(1994) and The Missing Head of Damasceno Monteiro *(1997).*

tle old ladies full of complaints about how in their day things were entirely different but now the world seems to have gone crazy, and lo and behold, just like that, a phrase pops up and you decide that's the one, you extract it from the conversation like a surgeon using his forceps to grasp a piece of tissue and isolate it, for example: *my late husband, when we celebrated our silver wedding anniversary*, that's all you need, this is an excellent phrase to begin with, today's a Sunday in late spring, a flock of pigeons circles over the roof of the Duomo and then does an about-face, sketching a bright stain in the sky, too many pigeons in this piazza, they're dirty, but it's pleasant to see them, the important thing is not to look at the bearer of the phrase, it's a rule you like to follow sometimes, so you look at the pigeons, you raise your eyes above, that old lady could be anybody, besides you can imagine her, she's talking to the fellow at the newsstand, you've heard her ask for the radio schedule, what a lovely phrase to start off your game, you snip it out with your mental scissors, among other things the word *silver* forms a dream marriage with the bright stain sketched by the pigeons, you start crossing the piazza, the work of consolidation isn't yet finished, you repeat the phrase to yourself a couple times, you savor it, a good opener, like some decent cards in a poker game, who knows what you'll make of it tonight, the night's a perfect time to write an absurd yet logical piece bestowed on you by other people's voices, something that'll tell a story utterly different from the one the people you've stolen it from would tell and something that belongs to you alone, since they wouldn't know what to do with this story, they wouldn't even recognize it, they each furnished a little piece, a pebble you've collected, chosen, fitted into the place that suited it, that place and only that place, so as to build the mosaic you'll view tonight with eager eyes, amazed to see how things unfold, how one word is wedged next to another, one event next to another, one detail next to another, creating a situation that didn't exist but now exists: your story.

One idea might be to sit at a café on Piazza Dante, there's a pasticceria with a spread of tables outside, in front of a little shop called La Rapida where shoes and bags are repaired, at this hour some customers are always there eating ice cream or drinking coffee, on such a lovely afternoon the elderly men who live in the hovels around the piazza have also come out, always wearing hats, spitting frequently, playing cards, every so often muttering things that are nearly incomprehensible, talking to other people as if they were talking to themselves, it's their way of communicating something to somebody, they present an ideal opportunity to find a phrase like the one you've already collected, let's see what you can put together. You head down Via Santa Maria, the first flocks of tourists mill about, cameras hanging from their necks, some take photos, from here the tower offers a strange perspective, you can see a crooked bit that looks as if it might tumble onto the roofs, it makes a certain impression, a boarding school for nuns once stood on the site of this snack bar, it always comes to mind when you pass by, you used to go there to meet a girl called Cristina, an eternity ago, you haven't the slightest desire to figure out when, you were someone else at that point, how strange, but the memory stayed with you, with the person you are now. *He gave out that he was dead to avoid the shame of failure.* This is a gift, you don't even have to isolate it from the other sentences, since the chatter of the two ladies who passed by you has already grown faint, two meters away, you turn around to look at them, breaking the rules, you see only that one lady's face wears an expression of utter astonishment, as if she couldn't believe her ears, and the other one is nodding as if to say, this is just how it is, my dear, believe me; they're elegant women who are probably going to mass at the Duomo, the mass is later, but they'll spend the afternoon people-watching, gossiping, sharing confidences, who knows whom they were discussing, what man might've feigned his death to avoid so much shame, anyway it makes no difference to you, the important thing is that now the story's opening has a continuation that's really promising: my late husband, when we celebrated our silver wedding anniversary, gave out that he was dead to avoid the shame of failure. There's even a hint of assonance, it doesn't hurt. For now you can tack on a period and wait for what destiny brings you.

What a pity the weather is suddenly changing. A strong wind has risen, in gusts, cool and brackish, coming from the sea, the light has turned gray, as if a storm were imminent, and by noon a wall of inky clouds has been erected, enhancing the marble of the bridges and the church of the Spina which now seems like a fragile vessel painted on a glittering backdrop. There's electricity in the air, you feel it, the slightest sensitivity to these things is sufficient, you notice it in the pigeon's restless flight, in the unnatural way people are rushing around, in the edginess of the cats in the piazza, you know it quite well, you completely understand this place and its climate, when a spring storm arrives from the sea it takes at least two hours to build over the city, before lightning flashes on the horizon with a rumbling of thunder like cannons in the distance; then the clouds arrive dense, like blocks without cracks, leaden; the city darkens, night falls in the middle of the day, and only at that point is the storm unleashed, with devastating wind and rain falling aslant, in squalls, implacable.

At Café Dante they're prudently removing the tables and stacking them indoors, one on top of the other, against the liquor boxes in the corner, so the customers won't be disturbed. You order a coffee and hang around a little while, listening to the remarks made by the owner and his friend about the news coming over the radio, the football matches under way. The Roman team Juventus is losing and no one expected it, what with that squad from the provinces; it's because of the playing field, argues the café owner, it's like a swamp; but it's a swamp for the other team too, the friend rightly objects; yeah, says the owner, except the champions are at a disadvantage on a muddy field, you know how delicate they are, they play on their toes, like ballerinas from La Scala, you can't make a ballerina from La Scala dance on a sidewalk. The friend nods, not very convinced, then says: bah, what crazy weather, it looks bewitched; he goes to look out the glass door and shakes his head, this must be because it's a leap year, he says conclusively, every leap year seems to be like this.

You take your cup of coffee into the adjoining room, where the regulars are playing cards. It's always the same ones, you've known them for years, and they recognize you, they know you come there to watch them play, or at least that's what they think, and they tolerate your presence, although it's a known fact that card players detest having curious onlookers around them. But between you and them there exists almost a complicity, as if you were old friends, even if you aren't friends, scarcely acquaintances, they don't even know your name, but it doesn't matter, it's enough to greet each other cordially: buona sera, how's the game going, you old incorrigibles? Someone smiles, someone else shakes his head, another lifts a hand to make a gesture of feigned protest; so you look around, sipping your coffee, undecided about which table to pick. The one in the back has a dramatic poker game, better not sit there; at the one near the door there's a rather animated game of scopone; at another table sits an elegant group playing briscola a cinque, a strange game, a mixture of chance and cunning, a little like your game with words, you need to pick among the cards that chance allots you and on the basis of them guess your partner, because you have a partner and you must guess who it is among four possible partners, you must rely on fate and intuition, this game is fine, you approach a chair and start watching in silence, your eyes attending to the cards, your ears attending to the phrases that hover in the room, sibylline phrases, from the players: a few curses, words whose value lasts an instant and then vanishes, driven out by other words.

I could never tell you before, but now you need to know. The sentence suddenly reaches your ears with the shock of a sudden wound from a needle or a drill, then you feel it explode inside your head and echo at intervals before fading away: *you need to know.* You've leapt to your feet, watching the door as if you're being hunted, the players are looking at you, you must've blanched, your eyes must be fearful, you sit down, trying to appear nonchalant, alright, no one's

paying attention to you anymore, they probably thought
your bizarre behavior was provoked by boredom; you look
at every player, one by one, you think about which of them
might've been the source of that voice, if it were in fact any
of those present, you think again of the voice, still resounding in your ears, it's unmistakable, nasal, with a slight drawl
and a note of irony in the tone, it's a voice you've known
too well; then, very softly, as if to yourself, you say: Tadeus,
you're here, I heard you, tell me where you're hiding. You
look again at the players, that little old man with the beret
and the haggard look, was it him? you think, did Tadeus
speak to me through him? And then the others: a corpu-
lent fifty-year-old with a tranquil air, two young men with
brilliantined hair, the four middle-aged gentlemen playing
poker; no, you think, it isn't any of them, Tadeus is here,
no doubt, this is where he's wandering about, but where
exactly? You start looking around the room, object by
object, how absurd, as if Tadeus's presence could be hidden inside every object: the calendar on the wall, with a
reproduction of a painting by the realist Giovanni Fattori,
the oleograph next to the mirror, where you can see a
hunter shooting a moor hen, the chandelier of fake crystal
with the bell-shaped lampshades, and you repeat: Tadeus,
please, I heard you; what do you want to tell me? from
where are you speaking to me? it isn't possible, you aren't
here any longer, your voice can't be here. Meanwhile your
mind repeats: from where are you speaking to me, Tadeus,
what do you want to tell me? And how strange: you understand perfectly that the voice isn't there any longer, it won't
speak to you again through the beings in that room, you
have to search for it, pursue it outside, when the opportu-

nity presents itself; then you stand up, give a distracted wave goodbye, now your mind's empty, you've thrown away the sentences you gathered during the day, only one voice remains inside you, precise and strong, and it says, *I could never tell you before, but now you need to know.*

What could you never tell me before? This is what you repeat to yourself as you leave the café uncertain about which direction to take, what couldn't you tell me before? And now you're speaking in a loud voice, because two passersby turn around to look at you, now you're furnishing others with ready-made phrases. You've got to calm down, you feel it, you've got to sit and think, pick a bench in the park, the sky is increasingly growing dark, you start to think about those years, all of them, it's impossible to think about all of them at once, you've got to take things in order, but do things have an order? And to what order does such a sentence refer? To what time, what moment, what situation? To all of them, it can refer to all of them, therefore it's useless to think about things in order, let them come just as they come. You think: it refers to the novel, that novel with the terrible ending. Was it merely your fault or did something work in such a way as to give that novel a terrible ending? Perhaps something *worked in such a way*, but what? Now you've really got to think, you'd probably have to reconstruct everything in minute detail, those moments, that unfortunate summer, the storms in September, the solitary evenings, the villa, Isabel who always wanted someone over to supper, she was frightened, perhaps, those evenings frightened her, and the novel had a terrible ending. But no, the novel has nothing to do with it, she was simply left to her fate, because it was right that she be. But was it right to throw away a living creature in that manner? It wasn't right, you know it, she was only a scapegoat, a strange vendetta. You hear the nocturnal wind again, when the storm was raging and the old windows creaked; Isabel never noticed anything, anything that might concern the novel, she never attached any importance to it, she only made sure she had company, she didn't want to be alone with you in that frightening house on the cliff. Then, with a transition that seems incongruous but to you is very logical, you say: Isabel was unhappy, her fear was principally this. You're saying this to the white grand duke who rises over the piazza surrounded by the Pompeian red houses, it's the piazza you love most in the entire city, with an unusual geometry, cut into a trapezoid by a palazzo with bulging iron bars; the sky is livid, the grand duke looks toward the sea, as if he fears the storm and watches for its arrival; she was just unhappy, I was mistaken, believing she was afraid, or better, this too is a way of being afraid, because unhappiness is a form of fear. You go sit on a stone plinth, absurdly hoping that the statue with the realistic features might bring you a voice that is now avoiding you; but then why shouldn't it? It's a horseman with a long cloak, his face noble and sad; he must've known the taste of power and the bitterness of betrayal, perhaps even he could bear the voice to you; and so you sit, light a cigarette, look at the horseman from top to bottom, his horse seems to hesitate amid the clouds, it's a charger that in its huge empty eye sockets carries the same amazement and the same sadness as his knight, you say: Tadeus, please, what do you have to tell me? Meanwhile you think again about that summer you had so carefully forgotten,

stowing it away in a vault on which you laid a heavy cover.
And now that cover, as if by magic, has moved, slipped
aside, opening a crack; you take a deep breath because a
scent of lavender reaches you, the land around the villa was
full of lavender, the morning when you went down to the
cliff, the air smelt of salt and shrubbery; then you turn
back because a cry came from the house, no, it's like a
muffled scream, a sob that the wind brings you, you're
uncertain about whether to head back, but you don't want
to know, nothing happened, it's just something that happens every so often, a sob, and then you repeat: unhappiness is a form of fear, Tadeus, I've always known it but I
never wanted to think about it, is this what you want to
remind me of, do you want to speak to me about Isabel, is
this why you're calling me? But the grand duke looks
toward the sea with his empty eyes, now the clouds have
started to gallop setting his charger galloping as well, as if
they were flying away together toward their past, they too
moving in the opposite direction; and so you stand up and
cross the piazza you've crossed so many times in your life,
you still remember the old cinema that burned down, they
took you there as a child to see Charlot, you walk along the
Arno and lean against the parapet, toward the mouth of
the river a blade of ominous violet light has opened, more
people are here, you think quickly about where to go, he
wants to talk to you, his voice needs a voice, or more precisely, it's you who want him to talk to you now: you must
talk, Tadeus, you can't say something like this and just leave
it hanging; where are you, the city is big, are you here or
waiting for me somewhere else? If you're here follow me,
please, let's go find a place where people are talking, tell me

again, I need you to talk to me again, you can't stop at this point. What frightened you? Or *who*? I can't avoid formulating this thought, you understand me, Tadeus, it's you who made me think about it, look, I wouldn't have wanted it, I swear to you, for years I didn't want to think about it, but now you've forced me, because one can't be afraid of just a place, a house, you're afraid of someone or something, I tell you because that day I kept away, I stayed on the cliff the whole day, I did it so I wouldn't know, I can't explain it any other way, why else would I stay on the cliff for the entire day? I heard the muffled scream and turned around to look, a car stood in front of the villa, it wasn't yours, it was an unfamiliar car, I should've gone to see, but Isabel didn't want me to know either, and so I passed the time by looking at the sea, with a sense of loss and futility, waiting for everything to happen, but you know everything, Tadeus, and now you've got to tell me. You've got to tell me because otherwise . . .

Otherwise what? Does your threat have any meaning? In your heart you know very well that it means nothing at all, since you could also insult him, curse him, but wherever he is, he's laughing at your curses. He's already in the realm of the cursed, you've always known it, and now he's laughing at you who would like to augur his hell; he is completely at his leisure in a place for which he's been preparing his whole life, a life composed of denial and dissipation, spent in thinking ill of himself and others, wholly dedicated to tempting and being tempted. You also know that you are now tempting yourself. His invitation, crafty and malicious, is in its way a challenge, a temptation, and you say: Tadeus, that day you arrived in another car, you intended to convince Isabel to do something, you saw to everything, plotted everything, organized everything, you were preparing for your perdition.

And how did he prepare for it? you're thinking at this hour as you the cross the Lungarno toward the fort, a part of the city where the palazzos grow sparse near the old crenellated walls covered with trails of ivy, the wind has now turned furious, it blows in gusts and sends leaves and old newspapers whirling into the air, how did he prepare for that perdition, how did he trick his victim? You see him again, with his ironic smile and his ready answers, witty, anticonformist, sarcastic: really amusing, Tadeus, heartfelt friend, in fact, thought-provoking friend, since it was to the intellect that he attached so much importance, intelligence was his badge. And Magda, you think, what role did she play in this story? So quiet and so solicitous, so available, nearly obliging, with her languid eyes and her eternal nostalgia for something she seemed to have lost, although just what it might've been was never clear: what was your part, Magda? Beyond the gate of the old walls, in front of the barracks and behind the athletic field, stands the bar called the Rondinella Sport Club, that's where you unconsciously direct your steps as you answer that Magda played the love interest, yes, in her way it was love, even if ill placed, even if with negative consequences; you turn the door handle, the place is filled with utter confusion, smoke, noise; some little boys, dressed as if they were about to play football, in jerseys and shorts, wait for the Sunday match to begin, but apparently this is the subject of differing opinions, given the bad weather, the parents accompanying them would prefer that the game be postponed, a father dressed as a referee looks perplexed, doesn't know what to decide, listens to the opposing sides trying to find a solution, the Rondinella Club boys await the outcome of the discussion, seem unconcerned, sit on benches and drink orangeade; the visiting team seems more brave, they've come from another city and risk making the journey in vain, among them is a particularly excited little boy with number eleven on his jersey, he can't stay still a minute, paces up and down among his mates, says: we've got to play the game, what else have we come to do; you look at him a moment, he's thin, freckled, his eyes blaze, and at that point, just for you, he opens his mouth to speak to his mates and brings you an unequivocal voice, nasal, slightly ironic, roaring in your ears as if it were shouted from a loudspeaker: *something that you too can discover; all you need do is prick up your ears at the highest point in the city.* You wait a few seconds in the hope that the communication might continue, but now the boy is speaking in his shrill little boy's voice, the din of voices is rekindled around you, and you hurl yourself outside as if by instinct, some huge raindrops are already falling and the wind is very strong, beneath the bar's awning stand a cluster of fans in heated debate, some maintain that the game must be postponed, others that this must be disputed in every possible way, among the latter is a big fat guy who demands they be silent and pointing to the poster affixed to the door he reads in a loud voice, in support of his point, the date of the match: the 10th of May at 6 p.m. The voice in which he reads is a voice that leaves no room for doubt, you recognize it even in its most subtle nuances; and then you immediately look at your watch, because by now the message is clear, as clear as the appointment, it's twenty-five minutes to six and the tower is far away, at the end of the street that runs around the perimeter, that's the highest point in the city, that's where he wants you to go so that you might know.

But know what? you still have the strength to murmur as you break into a run; you could try to wait for a bus, but today's Sunday and they're on a reduced schedule, better not take any risks, if you run you can make it, you haven't run like this in a long time, your head's starting to throb, your heart's beating fast, you're forced to slow down, but it's alright, the road is starting to go downhill. To save time you go around the ugly building that houses the Faculty of Pharmacy, cross the gardens and come out again on the street, the branches of the linden trees are violently shaken by the wind, a yellowish carpet of pollen has formed on the ground making it slippery, this forces you to stick close to the houses and meanwhile you say: it wasn't my fault, I didn't know anything. Then you look at your watch, because you've sighted the piazza, the broad expanse of grass beneath the arched gate, and now you know you can make it, you've got more than fifteen minutes. A few souvenir stalls are still open, many dealers hurried to close shop for fear of the storm. The piazza is nearly deserted, you shoot past a little group of American ladies wearing see-through raincoats, they've gotten off a bus and are taking photos of the tower; you cut across the lawn, the grass is drenched and it soaks your shoes but you don't notice, you're already at the door of the tower, luckily no people are waiting in line at the ticket office, you buy a ticket, panting, the ticket seller looks at you perplexed, you try to appear nonchalant and fix your hair, then you walk calmly toward the stairs because you feel the ticket seller is observing you with too much curiosity and you don't want to arouse his suspicion. As soon as you've taken the first flight of stairs, however, you pick up the pace again, you're sweating profusely, the tower stairs are terrible, steep and sloping, a winding staircase, like a bowel, and at every turn you see the city descending lower through the large windows, first the roofs of Via Santa Maria, then the ring of walls, then the river passing through the city with two wide bends, you emerge on the first landing, four minutes before six, at this point there's only one flight of stairs, the one that leads to the landing with the bells, you slip through the narrow opening of the door, you feel your legs giving way, but now you're here, you enter the last gallery and look out onto the city. There are only two stubborn tourists, a middle-aged couple who gaze at the panorama with binoculars, at first sight they look like foreigners, you approach unobtrusively, perch on a parapet at a distance that allows you to pick up their conversation, they've lowered the binoculars and chat, she ties a kerchief around her head for protection, the dark clouds have now descended over the entire city, they're speaking French, a few fragmentary sentences, it's an illness that can be controlled today, he says, a virus similar to herpes zoster. Then they fall silent, take one another's hands and head down the stairs. You look around amazed, no one has remained, you're alone, up there at the top, you feel betrayed, you say: Tadeus, you have falsely made an appointment with me. And at that moment the rain bursts into a violent downpour, a flash of lightning sketches a zigzag on the river, the swollen clouds open and the city cowers beneath the downpour. You calmly let yourself get

soaked, you grasp the iron bar on the parapet and suddenly
the largest bell begins to strike six, it tolls deep and dark
making the floor vibrate, the entire tower seems to shake,
you look into the distance, toward the sea, and then
beneath you, straight down. You feel the dizziness seize
your gaze and transform into a chill that runs down your
back and arrives at your hands which open and close by
themselves on the iron bar of the parapet: now you know
why Tadeus summoned you thus far; no one but he could
have made such an appointment with you.

(1991)

The Air of Rome
(An Old Man's Story)
Lalla Romano

SHE WAS ALMOST THREE YEARS older than me. She was beautiful and didn't give a damn about it. I really liked this about her; women who are too feminine always rubbed me the wrong way. But I also knew how risky her attitude might be: in a woman it allowed for a great deal of open-mindedness, indifference, even self-contempt. Maybe this side of her, which in my eyes made her seem pathetic, defenseless, influenced my decision never to take advantage of the fondness she showed toward me. It soon evoked in me a feeling of expectation as well, because after I'd known her for a few months I asked her to marry me. (I was a student, the eldest of five brothers, and this plan

LALLA ROMANO *(1906–2001) was born in Cuneo. She began her career as a poet, but in 1951 she published the first of many auto-biographical narratives. Her evocative writing, long neglected by English-language translators, treats such themes as the German occu-pation and relations between parents and children. Her novel* The Gentle Words Between Us *(1969) won the prestigious Strega Prize. In this story, she adopts a male persona to sketch a trip to Rome taken by a Piemontese couple during the Fascist period.*

smacked of sheer madness.) She answered me with a shrug, which in her language might be a yes or a no; but she agreed to go out with me several times, in quick succession, and told me all about herself.

The idea of a trip to Rome was mine, since she didn't express any preferences or make any plans. She said, in fact, that she felt better with me than with her usual partners (intellectuals) because they never took the initiative.

When we were about to leave, my firm resolve did not diminish the intoxicating sense I had of being on a honeymoon—and a secret one, to boot!

We had tickets in third class. We found ourselves in an empty compartment. I hugged her without kissing her. I couldn't stay still. I went to get pillows, then newspapers, then some oranges; and every time I walked the length of the train, I got off and hoisted myself onto the car with a single leap. I carefully arranged our things on the rack, and even our third-class refuge seemed like a good thing to me.

At Alessandria an old woman boarded with a young man who appeared to be her son. They sat in front of us and started talking very closely in low voices, interrupting each other with snickers that made the woman's plump belly jump. We stared at them and broke off our conversation. I suspected something indecent in their talk; every so often the woman would look at us with the kind glances of an old peasant, half stupid and half cunning.

Anna still didn't know me very well if she expected that my practical bent would lead me to switch off the light without knowing what the others might think of it. She didn't ask me, and it was the young man who at a certain point stood up. In the darkness the old woman took off her shoes and planted her short knobby feet on the seat next to me. I tried to overcome my disgust and smiled at her, as if I had approved the thing.

Anna leaned her head on my shoulder; it began to sway back and forth, to roll on my chest. I supported her by sitting up straight, as I had already done so many times on the way back from the ski runs. When I felt that she was really asleep, I laid her on the wooden seat, covered her with overcoats, and sat in front of her, next to the other two who were also sleeping. I looked at her and couldn't understand how she was able to sleep on a trip like that. But her nonchalance made me like her even more.

At Pisa the train stopped for an eternity. The old woman and young man had gotten off. I was standing, but I didn't dare abandon Anna. In the silence, a voice rose, very near by, in the next compartment. A woman's voice, clear, mellow. It evoked a mature woman with soft, white skin, a woman who was certainly beautiful. A deep, masculine voice responded briefly to her. When I grasped the words, I was shocked. The woman's voice was imbued with a languor I had not noticed before; and what she said was upsetting to me (I was twenty). She said, "My husband and I don't get tired so fast." And then, what was more terrible, she laughed. "Even when we stay in bed all night and the day after." She was laughing gently, pleased. I was indignant that a woman would talk to a stranger about her relations with her husband; but precisely for this reason (as I now realize) the unknown woman was immensely desirable to me. I went so far as to imagine, for a moment, that the man she was with had gotten off the train and I approached her while Anna slept. I watched Anna sleep, her thin white face tinged violet in the half-light. With her eyes closed, she seemed remote, cold.

At dawn the train picked up speed. Anna, now awake, began to ruffle her hair. Every so often a few strands would tickle my face. The car had filled—men and women with baskets of produce and hens: it was market day at Grosseto. A blind man sang, accompanying himself on an accordian. His head was egg-shaped, shaven like a prisoner's, and he swayed it to the rhythm of his songs. The noisy meter of the train didn't bother him, even though it beat out a tempo much more rapid than his.

We were already familiar with Rome, me because I'd lived there as a child, Anna because she'd visited it to take a national examination (she'd gotten her degree two years before). At the Villa Borghese I would support her because she walked around looking overhead. The pine trees and the air of Rome were rather exotic for us, but not so much as to be bewildering.

To eat, the thing to do was to go to Trastevere; we preferred native Rome. It was in fact Anna who made this suggestion, which was unusual, a sign that she was happy. In one of those sunny streets, we found a small, dark trattoria. From the table we saw the facing wall, deteriorating, gold-colored. A horse beat its hooves on the cobbles.

Two men came in together, huge and noisy, bricklayers. They started eating heads of lettuce. We northerners sat bolt upright and watched them, enchanted.

The people amused Anna, and the wine, and then— could a twenty-year-old understand? Was she herself aware of it?—something had transformed her. She looked me in the eyes, laughing for no particular reason as if she were making fun of me. She aroused me, and her playfulness was so new that I desired her more than ever, although in a frenzy.

I left, pulling her by the hand as she laughed. We walked in the sun, nearly running, I was dazed—and I hadn't drunk anything—she seemed tipsy, loose. All we needed was to be approached by one of those little old men who offer rooms. But it didn't happen.

We gradually became more light-footed: she too, I believe. I wasn't looking at her; she was still laughing, or whining.

We entered the Archaeological Walk. The gates of the Baths were closed. We stopped there, a bit out of breath. We stood in the cool shade of the high walls. No one was there. But it wasn't a complicit solitude, it was austere, as in the mountains or in a church.

That whole site was in fact a cross between a dilapidated church and a mountain ravine: sumptuous, despite everything. It would have been beautiful to stroll around inside there precisely because it was incomplete, full of air, of sky.

We searched for someone who could tell us when they would open. A long way off in the sunlight we saw a carabiniere's silhouette, tiny and droll. We could ask him. He was slowly walking toward us. When he was close, you could see that he was reading, holding right in front of his face a large book with a broken binding, a novel in the style of Eugène Sue, from which a poppy dangled as a bookmark. He lifted his head: he had a child's face, red, pockmarked. His little eyes almost closed when he smiled. He shrugged.

Slowly, in the calm, scorching afternoon, we resumed

wandering. The road climbed a hill between walls over-grown with wild greenery. A gate was open: Villa Celi-montana. There too silence enveloped everything, yet a silence that was gentle, pleasant, with rustling pines and occasional voices, slow and clear, women we couldn't see. We sat on a bench in the shade. Beyond lay the sun-filled meadow, with low, dark hedges. A child passed by, running between them.

In that state of surrender—we had grown silent—suddenly the woman on the train crossed my mind. A nocturnal shadow fell on the pines and the sky. I looked at Anna, her parted lips, and she in turn looked at me. We closed our eyes and our lips joined like someone thirsty at a fountain spout. The crunch of the gravel roused us. It was a policeman. "Stand up." Only I stood. I think I was trembling. He wrote our names in a notebook, spelling them out. "You are under arrest." "You'll ruin me." Anna stood, tore some leaves from a hedge, chewed them and then spat them out. I wasn't looking at her, naturally, but I saw her. I put all the money I had into the policeman's hand. He took it a moment as if to weigh it, then gave it back to me. I nodded at the page with the names; he removed it and handed it to me. I tore it up and thrust it into my pocket. I took Anna by the hand and we left, heading down the tranquil road, running as if we were being pursued.

Far away, while we were catching our breath, I tore the page into smaller pieces, put them back into my pocket, and said, "We found a good man." Anna railed at me; I let her talk. She said things against the cops, the Regime, Rome, things I'd said a hundred times. I knew her rage was a way of venting her fear and especially the weight of the day; perhaps, underneath, there were also hard feelings against me (although not for the reason she thought). But whether she understood didn't matter to me. I sensed there was something else I couldn't grasp, because it was a woman's reaction. At a certain point, in fact, she said, "He made everything dirty." I smiled, and this exasperated her. I also felt a bit detached from her; hadn't I been thinking much more about myself when I was trying to persuade the policeman?

We arrived at the top of the Janiculum. Anna sat on a little wall; her feet were raw after so much running. Rome appeared golden, at sunset, and the Altar of the Nation gleamed white, like sugar. Behind stood a wooded green plot; you could see a flock grazing and, deep in the wood, a small classical pediment, something suggestive of Poussin. (Gone now, I suppose.) We were doing so well there, made slightly melancholy by the beauty, that my vigilance had again relaxed. We crossed a clearing covered with gravel and went down without hurrying. Voices suddenly nearby, at our backs, made us turn round; a group of policemen were following us, carrying their bicycles. They followed us in the sense that they came behind. Conceited, self-assured, they were talking among themselves, laughing loudly. Anna grabbed my hand, but I didn't repulse her; I indicated that we shouldn't run. We were last; they were already closing the gates.

Later, at a restaurant, we couldn't stop laughing, but we felt safe only when we found the train schedule and decided the time of our departure.

We waited to leave in a café. A cold wind had risen, and it blew inside as well, through the open door. The mirrors returned our images with the slightly downcast look of "after the fall." But we no longer had any desire to laugh. To kiss, yes, but for us even the café was guarded by a policeman's flaming sword.

We boarded the train when it was still empty and dark. I fell asleep first; I must have slouched against her, and she then leaned on me, and we traveled this way, like worn-out children. We awoke at the same time, and we saw that our fellow travelers were gazing tenderly at us. We were stuck in an uncomfortable position, stinking of the train, but we felt connected like an old couple.

Outside was the dawn. The train sped along the sea. The sea was an eye, clear and deep—the eye of God?—watching us.

Inland, as we approached home, we turned sad again: we were about to separate. Without speaking, we watched the landscape draw near and flee. The familiar, humble landscape: the mulberry trees, useful and inelegant; the land, tilled, red; the salad greens, ingenuously shrill.

For us, at that moment, no sight could have been more consoling.

(1975)

The Lady with the Fan

Aldo Palazzeschi

FOR THREE CONSECUTIVE NIGHTS during the full moon in August, the figure of a lady covered almost completely by a large red fan was seen at the top of the Colosseum.

The lights at ground level joined with the floodlights overhead to display the huge size and vivid color of the fan, while the moon's brightness, neutralized in that illumination, cast the woman's body in shadow so that no one managed to see her clearly.

On the third night two police officers dashed to the top of the Colosseum to confirm this presence and to gather information from the said lady regarding her nocturnal predilections. While they were breathlessly climbing, the lady disappeared, and it proved impossible to track her down.

ALDO PALAZZESCHI *was the pseudonym of Aldo Giurlani (1885–1974), who was born in Florence but lived in Venice and Paris before settling in Rome. A member of the Futurist movement, he wrote experimental poetry. His fiction displays his satirical bent. English translations of his work include the novel,* Perelà, Man of Smoke *(1911).*

The news spread through the city, and for several days there was talk of nothing else.

Was it a real apparition or an illusion, created and maintained by the natural and artificial lights which in that suggestive place conspired to work their sorcery?

A few nights later, the very same apparition was seen on the tower of the Campidoglio. From that symbolic point, the lady waved the large red fan as if she wanted to attract the attention of the entire metropolis and focus it on herself. And this time too, while the fan was clearly perceived, no one managed to discern the figure that was somehow shadowed by it. A custodian who climbed the tower, taking four steps at a time, reached the top to find nothing but ether and firmament.

Regarding this incident, many people affirmed that there was no lady, merely a fan, a large mechanical fan that waved through its own power on the edge of the Colosseum as well as on the tower of the Campidoglio. Others added, with greater competence and authority, that the fan was definitely of American manufacture, a little prodigy from the New World: *Made in U.S.A.*

A farmer who went to a market in the city to sell his produce reported that in the first dusky glimmers of dawn he had seen a lady sitting in the vicinity of Nero's grave, fanning herself with a large red fan. He stopped to see her better, but no sooner had he glanced at her than the woman fled, disappearing in the blink of an eye. Still, since she had to close the fan before fleeing, he could clearly see, first, her completely black face and, second, her red posterior, which shone almost as brightly as the fan.

However things stood, the lady was doubtless a for-

eigner, perhaps one who wanted to remain incognito after
arriving in Rome to learn about the city, or to enjoy herself, or merely to satisfy her curiosity.

Someone who very mysteriously boasted that he was
well informed in the matter took it for a fact that she was
an African princess who had come to Rome to visit Nero's
grave, even though she may have known that its site is still
in doubt.

Two police officers were stationed at the grave to
guard it.

Other people began to say that she was posing as a
tourist to conceal the most dreadful crime, and it was necessary to resolve the incident so as to check the flight of the
masses' morbid imagination and without delay rid the city
of the strange lady and her extraordinary fan. Whether or
not all these statements were true, from one day to the next
the lady's appearances were threatening to become a trou-
blesome problem.

The women of Rome were divided into two camps,
which grew more and more vast, unified, factious, and
impatient to enter the lists against one another. The first,
intransigent in the highest degree, demanded that wherever the now-famous lady was seen, she should be shot on
the spot. The opposing faction, however, considered this
demand terrible, barbaric, and crazy, because it endangered
the lives of innocent citizens and might result in an accident that would forever be a source of regret. The obvious
fact that the lady in question possessed a fan, a commonly
used object that one can find on sale everywhere, conferred
on her an aura of refinement, of coquetry, of feminine fascination which attracted and transported this second, more

receptive group of women, and so they expressed their unqualified admiration and active solidarity for the lady by asking for nothing more than to challenge her to a duel.

Yet there was greater cause for astonishment when a new rumor was added to the always-rising clamor and whispering. One night the lady with the fan had been seen driving through the narrow roads of the Villa Borghese in the embrace of a very young man who was possibly still in his teens. He had blond hair and was handsome in a delicate, charming sort of way. The car was moving very fast, and no one was able to read the license plate.

The young man was identified as the son of a well-known banker. When he was interrogated about the incident before the police commissioner, he declared that he had in fact driven through the Villa Borghese at that hour on that night, after leaving certain friends with whom he had eaten supper, but there was no lady in his car, neither a dark-haired nor a blond one, with or without a fan. He was driving there alone, very much alone.

As for the lady, even though the large fan may have covered her almost completely, on this occasion too it seemed certain that the color of her face was definitely black.

Every doubt was resolved: the lady was an African princess who had come to Rome to visit the city and perhaps make the acquaintance of some white citizens. There was, however, no new information regarding the problem of her posterior, and this aspect of the investigation did not make the slightest progress at all. The lady was sitting in a car, and the only reliable witness was the seat, but we all know that our current methods of investigation, while certainly antiquated and obsolete, no longer include the prac-

tice of interrogating seats. The omission of this practice
drew many complaints from the press.

The city dailies and the illustrated weeklies carried
drawings and ran very detailed reports with the most compelling particulars about the lady's private life. These
papers disagreed on various points, but on one they were
in complete agreement: they all made her face more or less
dark, its color ranging from the light brown of a mulatto
to the black of a negro from Senegal. They all pictured her
holding, with varying degrees of grace and guile, a large red
fan, and they vied with each other in reproducing its magnificence and in explaining its usefulness with a logic that
was no less than amazing. The lady was given to exasperated snobbery; since her arrival in Europe from the tropi-
cal regions, her sole preoccupation was with appearing to
suffer from the cold because she was now in a temperate
zone. If she constantly fanned herself, everyone would
think that she was undoubtedly a European woman
despite the color of her face.

It was not long before even more shocking news was
published to satisfy the voracious curiosity of the public.

The lady in question had been seen on the balcony of
the Quirinale, waving to a nonexistent crowd with her very
beautiful fan. Only one passerby happened to be crossing
the piazza at that moment, but it was impossible to get him
to estimate the size of the crowd. Nor could he say what
color the lady's face was. The metaphysical dimension of
that huge piazza, which is perhaps the most suggestive in
Rome when it contains a single citizen, had been trans-
mitted to his brain, producing there a magical void. He

swore again and again that on that balcony he had seen a lady who greeted him by waving a large red fan.

Porters and cuirassiers, carabinieri and policemen were all interrogated, but no one at any time had seen that lady enter the building. Every single door in the Quirinale was most carefully inspected; unless the lady had the power to render herself invisible at her pleasure and convenience, she had passed through none of them.

Her latest appearance further illuminated and documented one point alone. The idea that she stood on the balcony of the presidential palace to greet a cheering crowd, even if the piazza was deserted, proved beyond the shadow of a doubt the hypothesis that she was a royal princess—an African princess who had come on a private visit to the capital of Italy. And someone very appropriately added that she was a true and proper queen who, despite the highly private nature of her visit, did not depart from her customary practices and felt as familiar in that place as if she were at home.

When the president was interrogated, he declared that he had not received, either officially or in a private meeting, any princess or queen, whether she be white, black, gray, even yellow or green.

How could she have reached the balcony of the palace?

A new, thoroughly scientific investigation affirmed that the above-mentioned queen had reached the balcony of the Quirinale by nimbly climbing up a drainpipe and then proceeding along a cornice of the huge building. When the metaphysical citizen was asked for information about the queen's posterior, he broke his silence, obviously frightened, nearly offended. What could he possibly know about it if he hadn't even seen her face?

As far as the lady's posterior was concerned, the farmer who had surprised her near Nero's grave maintained his story, which, nonetheless, was to be accepted only with the greatest caution and concealed from the public until a more reliable testimony had been taken. The meeting had occurred in that dim light of daybreak, which seems designed especially to foster illusions. Notwithstanding this fact, the farmer was again interrogated.

"Are you really sure about it?"

"Very sure."

"Keep in mind that the issue of the lady's posterior is of inestimable interpretive value. Did you see it clearly? Can you describe it with precision? In that most deceptive and uncertain light, did you not fall victim to an error, a blunder?"

"There was no error, no blunder. I saw it very clearly as soon as she stood up to hurry away, and I still believe I saw it."

"Was it red?"

"Flaming."

"And shiny?"

"Like a mirror."

"It must have been very ugly."

"Oh, very ugly!"

"And how did you react to it?"

"If my wife had a backside like that, I would've asked for our marriage to be annulled without giving it a second thought."

The front pages of the illustrated weeklies carried a

drawing of the queen who was spending her visit to the
Eternal City in such an extraordinary way. Her face was
very beautiful, even though it was as black as a chimney;
her head was crowned with a tiara of diamonds and
pearls, which made her height seem superhuman; and a
mass of gold necklaces studded with gems descended
from her neck to her knees. She wore a white satin dress
decorated with silver elephants and a purple cloak on
which the equatorial sun was embroidered in gold. The
red fan, which was growing larger and larger and becoming increasingly indispensable and legendary, was
astonishing.

At this point a new incident occurred.

An unusual lady accompanied by an elegant young man
was seen seated at a table in Doney's on the Via Veneto.
She was beautiful, even though no longer very young. And
she was fanning herself with a large red fan.

An officer on the investigative squad approached the
table and with due caution asked the lady to show him her
papers. She lived in a villa in Parioli, and her papers were
in order. Fearful of committing a blunder through an
excess of zeal, the officer did not think it appropriate to
proceed further and so contented himself with taking her
address. He was also inclined to be circumspect because
the young man who accompanied her had assumed an
offended attitude. One does not ask a respectable woman
for her papers in a public place. To justify his action, the
officer alleged that the error was caused by the coincidence of the fan, and the lady, who began waving it in a
broad arc, responded with the most clamorous laughter.

When the officer arrived at police headquarters and delivered his significant report, the commissioner said that another communication had just been received: at Caffè Rosati in Piazza del Popolo a lady had been seen fanning herself with a large red fan. And here the officer had been shrewd enough to merit the commissioner's praise: he had limited himself to asking the lady, with consummate gallantry, where she had acquired that most beautiful object. With the greatest solicitude, the lady gave him the name of a shop in Corso Umberto.

Nonetheless, the mere possession of a fan was not conclusive evidence. Both of the ladies who were questioned had faces that seemed to be made of milk and rose petals, and their complexions promised heavenly uniformity throughout the rest of their bodies, no part excluded.

The owner of the shop in Corso Umberto affirmed without hesitation that he had indeed sold fans not only to those two ladies, but to more than two hundred others within the past forty-eight hours. Then he opened a cabinet and showed that it was full of the said fans, adding that he had commissioned several thousand from artisans who were working day and night. His business sense had advised him that this investment would be a sure success. In fact, so many shop owners had felt the same way that a few hours later, in clothing stores throughout Rome, other ladies were seen caressing their beautiful faces with the breezes produced by large red fans. This situation rendered all investigation into the matter absurd, if not impossible. Facial color remained the only positive proof, since a verification a posteriori was held to be not only illegal, but inconclusive as well.

And when the use of a red fan had spread throughout the elegant sections of the capital and stretched as far as the most exclusive suburbs, the police commissioner announced that the difficult operation was completed and crowned with the most brilliant success. The lady with the fan was under arrest.

This news turned the entire city upside down.

The women who used red fans rose like vipers, proclaiming that it was an injustice, a disgrace, an oppression without comparison: to arrest a woman for the most innocent use of a fan!

Those of the opposing faction shouted that it was necessary to stand her up against the wall and shoot her, ipso facto, without a trial. She had caused an ignominious scandal; a special ordinance must be instituted to prohibit any woman from using a fan so that public order might be restored.

The first group of women grew more and more venomous, loudly demanding that they be allowed to see her, speak with her, know something about her life, hear her voice, see her fan, verify whether it was hers, whether it was the same as theirs, and ask her for her photograph and autograph. To police headquarters in Rome they sent masses of gladioli, orchids, and tulips, boxes of candy, bottles of champagne. And the more the opposing faction shouted that it was necessary to teach all these women a lesson because of their foolishness and frivolity and at least punish them with a stiff fine, confiscating each one of their notorious fans to destroy them in a bonfire, the more the others shouted about an unspeakable disgrace, vile cruelty, and injustice, gathering at rallies where they simultaneously waved red fans at arm's length.

Before the lady with the fan arrived at the place to which she was destined, the police commissioner of Rome, in consultation with the prefect, decided to satisfy public curiosity so as to soothe spirits and find among the factions an area of common agreement, a platform on which to initiate discussion. He wanted everyone to see her, recognize her, and spend some time with her, so he organized a charity ball in her honor at the largest and most luxurious hotel in the city.

The rooms overflowed with an elegant and most vivacious audience. A gradually increasing electricity charged the air, keeping the tense crowd at a fever pitch of excitement.

Precisely at midnight, a dark mass dropped with an airy lightness from a gallery and landed in the center of the room, producing an instantaneous movement: everyone stepped aside at the same time. And no sooner had that dark lady entered than Commissioner Confetti made his way through the crowd. When he had reached her and taken her by the hand with cavalier charm, he turned toward the audience and said, "Here is the lady with the fan."

A sudden fearful scream cleared the center of the room, and the crowd's astonishment gave way to an icy silence. Everyone stared at the sinister figure who aroused so much uneasiness as to block any words, any movement. Finally, a brave woman broke the silence, which had now become offensive, and shamelessly said, "And why doesn't she have it?"

"Have what?" asked Commissioner Confetti.

"Her fan."

Not knowing what to answer, Commissioner Confetti looked at his companion, who gave him a slightly ironic smile.

"I left it home because I knew I'd find so many of them here. I'm an ape, as you can see, but if you look carefully, I'm the only one who isn't holding a fan."

Then she turned to the gentleman who accompanied her.

"And now we're off to the zoo. Commissioner, give me your arm."

But as if remembering something, she took a few steps and stopped, turning again to the audience.

"Before I leave, I'd like to do a little something that's easier for me than for you."

She bowed down to the floor, suddenly stuck out her tail, and showed what none of the women wanted to see— it was flaming red!

"Look."

They all covered their faces with their large red fans.

(1957)

The Thinker
Alberto Moravia

AT MARFORIO, a typical Roman restaurant in Traste-vere, everything went just fine in the beginning. My head was empty and resonant, like those shells you find at the seashore where the worm that crawled inside so long ago wound up dying. When customers ordered "spaghetti al sugo," my head would faithfully echo "spaghetti al sugo"; when they ordered "zuppa inglese," my head would always echo "zuppa inglese." No more, no less. In plain words, I wasn't thinking at all; I was a waiter inside and out. I was so much a waiter that at night, when I'd be dropping off to sleep, my head still reverberated with the various orders I'd taken all through the day. I said my head was empty, but it would be more true to say my head was frozen, like a mountain lake where the ice turns back to water in the

ALBERTO MORAVIA, *the pseudonym of Alberto Pincherle (1907–1990), was born in Rome where he lived throughout his life. A prolific writer of novels and short stories, Moravia sought to depict the various groups that comprise modern Roman society. English translations of his work are currently being reprinted, including such novels as* The Conformist *(1951) and* Contempt *(1954), both of which have been powerfully adapted to the screen.*

spring sunshine and one fine morning it starts moving again, rippling in the breeze. For sure, whether my head was empty or frozen is immaterial; what I really mean is, I was the perfect waiter, so perfect that once I heard a girl in the restaurant tell her friend as she pointed at me, "Look at that waiter there: he's got a waiter's face. He couldn't be anything but a waiter. He was born a waiter and he'll die one." I'd love to know what a waiter's face looks like. Most likely it's the kind of face that pleases customers, the kind they don't need to have because they don't need to please anybody, while waiters, if they want to keep on being waiters, need to have a waiter's face. You get my drift. For a solid year I never thought at all; I just filled the orders that customers gave me. Even when a customer acted out of line and shouted at me, "Are you an idiot or what?" my head would faithfully echo, "Are you an idiot or what?" No more, no less. Of course, the owner of the restaurant was happy with me. He would often tell the others, "I don't want any complaints. Follow Alfredo's example. He never speaks out of turn. He's a real waiter."

It started one night, just like the ice melting in the sunlight, turning back to water, moving with the current. An old, gargantuan customer, his head covered with graying curls as if sprinkled with snow, his dark face resembling a goat's—this guy started giving me a hard time, maybe to impress the girl he was with, some petty little blond, some typist or shop clerk. He was never satisfied, and when I brought him the dish he ordered, he began to grumble, "What's this stuff? . . . What kind of place is this? I don't know who they think I am to put this in front of me." He was wrong: he had asked for oxtail stew, and that's what I brought him. Except this time, instead of echoing his words in my usual way, I found myself saying silently: "Look at this fool's goat face." It wasn't an earth-shattering thought, I admit, but to me it was important because this was the first time I had actually thought ever since I started waiting on tables. Then I went to the kitchen, changed the plates, brought back two portions of lamb alla cacciatora, and thought again, "Tuck in, buster, and may you choke on it!" Another thought, you'll notice, and this one wasn't exactly a stroke a genius either, but a thought it was, nonetheless.

From that night on I started to think, I mean I started to do one thing while thinking of another, which is, I believe, what's usually called thinking. For instance, I'd bow down to ask, "Your order, Signori?" while inside I thought, "Check out the long neck on this fop. He looks like a goose." Or else I'd say with over-the-top attentiveness, "Cheese, Signora?" while instead I thought, "You've got a moustache, baby doll. You're bleaching it, but anybody can still see it." Most of the time, however, my head swarmed with threats and scurrilities, obscenities and insults: "Dunce, chump, asshole, freeloader, may your tongue shrivel up and your teeth rot," and so on. These words proved stronger than me; they were constantly boiling in my brain, like beans in a saucepan. Eventually I realized I was mentally concluding sentences I said aloud. If I asked, let's say, "Oil and lemon?" my inner voice would end the question with, "in your face, you stupid bastard?" Or I might ask, "Are you familiar with our specialties?" and end with, "Inedible slop at jacked-up prices." Now, I suddenly discovered I wasn't ending these sentences in my mind, but with my lips, even if in a softer tone, in fact so soft as to be inaudible. I was talking, to put it bluntly, although my speech still didn't exceed the bounds of prudence. To recapitulate: at first I didn't think at all, then I started to think, and now I was thinking out loud, or simply speaking.

I recall vividly what happened the first time I spoke. One Saturday evening, a couple who were obviously a Saturday-evening sort of couple went to sit at a table of mine. She must have been one of those women—a peroxide blond, brassy, stacked, tall, heavily made-up and reeking of perfume; he was a short, fair-haired guy with a red face, pointy nose, and curly hair, his shoulders were too broad, and he wore a blue suit, but with yellow shoes. She must have been from the north; he spoke with the closed "u" they use in Viterbo. He grabbed the menu as if it were a declaration of war and gave it a long, surly look, although without making a decision. Then he ordered a substantial meal for himself: spaghetti alla carbonara, lamb with potatoes, chicory salad dressed with oil, vinegar, and anchovies. She ordered things that were light, delicate. I scribbled down the orders in my notebook and headed for the kitchen. But as I set off, I couldn't help but glance back at him, and I noticed my lips said in a whisper, although distinctly, "What an ugly mug this guy has." He was still studying the menu and didn't catch it, but she, possessing the sharp ears typical of women, bounced on her chair and glared at me; she had heard. I went to the kitchen and shouted with as much volume as I could muster: "One consommé and one spaghetti alla carbonara." Then I returned to station myself against the wall a short distance away from them. Now she was laughing uncontrollably, pressing her hand against her chest, red in the face, and he was leaning toward her, irritated; he must have been asking her why she was laughing, but she just kept on laughing, shaking her head and pressing her hand against her chest. Finally she calmed down a bit, leaned toward him, and said something while pointing in my direction. He turned and looked squarely at me. I pretended to shift my gaze to another part of the room, and when I looked back at them, I saw she had started laughing again and he was staring at me, head lowered, like a ram about to charge, flashing his horrible eyes.

At length he called me, "Waiter." She stopped laughing, and I approached in no great hurry. As I approached, even though a little fearful, I couldn't help but murmur again, with conviction, "Yeah, he looks like a real lout." Then I presented myself with a "How can I help you?" and he raised his eyes toward me and said menacingly, "Waiter, a little while ago you expressed an opinion."

I pretended to be shocked. "An opinion? I don't understand."

"Yes, you delivered a judgment. The signora heard you."

"The signora did not hear correctly."

"The signora hears very well."

"I don't understand. Perhaps the gentleman no longer wishes the spaghetti. We can change the order."

"Waiter, you expressed an opinion and you know it." At this point, she leaned toward him and pleaded, "Look, it's better to let this pass." He then said, "Call the manager." I bowed and went to fetch the manager, who came, listened, spoke, debated, while she continued to laugh uncontrollably and her partner grew uglier than ever.

Then the manager came up to me and said in a low voice: "Now serve them and keep your mouth shut. If you do something like this again, you're fired."

"But I—"

"Not another word, troublemaker. Get going."

So I served them, in silence, but she kept on laughing through the entire meal, and he just picked at his food. In the end, they went away without having fruit—and without leaving a tip. But she kept on laughing, all the way to the door.

After that first incident, instead of mending my ways, I got worse. Now I had virtually stopped thinking; I merely spoke. During the day, when there were few people and the waiters stood idle among the tables or along the walls, I would mumble to myself, moving my lips, so that the others noticed it and asked me, laughing, "What are you doing? Saying your prayers? Reciting the rosary?" No, I wasn't praying, wasn't saying the rosary; I was rather looking at a family of five—father, mother, and three little ones—and murmuring, "He doesn't want to shell out because he's tightfisted or just doesn't have the cash. But she's an idiot with stars in her eyes and she's ordered the most expensive dishes: fresh vegetables, lobster, mushrooms, dessert. He's bent out of shape and fuming; she enjoys seeing him suffer, the wicked bitch. Meanwhile the kids are out of control, and he's having a rough time." Or I'd study the face of a customer with a huge wart sticking out from the top of his forehead. "Look at this potato head. It must feel strange to touch such a big wart. How does he wear a hat? Does he slip it over the wart or wear it on the back of his head?" In short, I was talking to myself, and the more I talked to myself, the less I talked in public. At the same time, the owner stopped referring to me as a model waiter; in fact, he would give me funny looks. I think he considered me a little crazy—and was waiting for the first opportunity to send me packing.

The opportunity arrived. One evening the restaurant was half empty, and the Trasteverine orchestra was playing "Anema e core" to the empty chairs. I turned round and yawned before a large table set for ten. The customers who had reserved it were not to be seen. I knew who they were, however, and my expectations weren't good. Finally they entered the brightly lit room, the women in evening dresses, animated, excited, speaking in loud voices, talking over their shoulders, and the men following them, all in dark blue, their hands in their pockets, bellies in the vanguard, at once flabby and vain. They were the so-called beautiful people; I'd once heard the term used by a fop who was gawking at them, "Did you see them? Tonight we dine with the beautiful people." Regardless of whether they were beautiful or ugly, I couldn't stand them for a load of reasons, the principal one being that they didn't address me formally, with the polite usages. "Bring me a chair . . . Give me the menu . . . Move it, come on, quick." They spoke to me with familiarity, as if we were brothers, and I didn't feel anybody was my brother, least of all any of them. True, they spoke with familiarity to everyone, to the other waiters, even to the owner, but this meant nothing to me; they could do it with God Almighty, if they wanted, but not with me, never. So they entered the restaurant, and the first thing they did was to start playing musical chairs. "Giulia, sit yourself there, Fabrizio there, Lorenzo next to me, I want Pietro here, Giovanna between us, Marisa at the end of the table." At last, as God wished, everyone found their seats, and I advanced with the menu, giving it to the man who sat at the head of the table, a fat, bald geezer with a walleye and a hawk nose, his throat pale and delicate, dusted with talcum powder.

"So, what do you recommend?" he asked.

It didn't sound as if he'd used the polite form, so I murmured, "Rat poison."

Luckily he didn't hear me because of the racket the others were making as they wrangled over the menu. Some wanted to eat spaghetti, others antipasto; some wanted Roman specialties, others said no; some wanted red wine, others white. The women especially were creating pandemonium, like so many hens shaking out lice in a chicken coop before going to sleep. I couldn't help but murmur through my teeth as I bowed behind him, "Just look at these cackling hens."

He must have heard me because he jumped and asked: "What did you say? Chicken?"

"Yes," I explained, "we have stewed chicken."

"What do you mean stewed chicken!" someone shouted. "We want to eat alla romana: broad beans with streaky bacon, pagliata."

"What exactly is pagliata?"

"Pagliata," said the man who was reading the menu, "is the small bowel of an unweaned calf who has never eaten grass, cooked with everything inside, in other words with the excrement."

"Excrement? How horrible!"

"That's what you should all be force-fed," I thought, or rather murmured as I bowed.

This time he heard something because he asked, almost incredulous, "What?"

"I didn't speak."

"You did speak, and you said something," he replied firmly, but still without anger. Meanwhile it had somehow grown silent, not only at that table, but throughout the restaurant. Even the orchestra happened to interrupt its playing. In this silence, I heard myself say in a low yet clear voice, "You can stuff the familiarity—and drop dead."

He immediately leaped up with amazing violence. "Me drop dead? Do you know who you're talking to?"

"I didn't say anything."

"Me drop dead? You scoundrel, I'll teach you." Now standing, he grabbed me by the collar and hurled me against the wall. The rest of the people at the table had also risen to their feet, and some were trying to restore peace while others were railing against me. At this point, the entire restaurant was staring at us. I was getting angry, and, pushing back, I told him, "I didn't say anything. Take your hands off me."

"Ah, so you didn't say anything?"

"I didn't say anything," I repeated, freeing myself from his grip. And then, in a lower voice, "Drop dead."

Thus the phrase escaped me a second time. Luckily the manager arrived at the right moment, pliant as a rush, obsequious as a snake. "Please, Commendatore, prego, prego." The Commendatore, typical of the vulgarian he was, shouted, "I'll break his face." The manager finally seized me by the arm, saying, "You come with me."

Here was the familiar address again. As we crossed the room, with all the people standing to see us better, I couldn't help but think out loud, "More of this familiarity. You can drop dead too." Then and there he said nothing, but as soon as we reached the kitchen and the door was closed, he screamed into my face, "So you tell the customers to drop dead and now you're telling me?"

"But I didn't say anything . . . Drop dead."

"And you still insist! It's you who've been dropped, my friend. Out you go, now!"

"Fine with me. I'm leaving. Drop dead."

My lips were moving against my will, and I could do nothing to stop them. I was standing in the street, protesting, although not quite out loud. "They speak to you with familiarity as if they're your brothers, and who's ever seen them before, who's ever met them? Why don't they keep the proper distance?"

At that moment a policeman, seeing that I was talking to myself, approached and questioned me, "Been drinking, eh? Is that how it is? A dry wine or medium? Move along, let's go. You can't stay here."

"Who's been drinking?" I protested. And immediately that phrase issued from my mouth, the same one that got me tossed from the Marforio. I'd have liked to nab it again, like a butterfly that slips out of a cap. But ah yes, it had escaped me, and there was nothing I could do about it now. So, I was arrested for insulting an officer, spent the night in lockup, was tried and put on probation. When I left the jailhouse, I noticed that my head was frozen again. Dazed, I crossed the street at the Vittorio Emanuele bridge when a car nearly ran me down. Although I was trembling, the driver wasn't satisfied; he leaned out the window and shouted at me, "Hey, buddy, you're braindead!" I watched him drive away as my head echoed faithfully, just like a year ago, "Braindead, braindead, braindead."

(1954)

The Game

Luigi Malerba

FIFTEEN YEARS OLD is a very uncertain and confused age. I see it in my son. He is always troubled, always absent-minded, as if he lived with his head in the clouds. Some days he sits in front of the television without switching it on and stays there for hours. I haven't the faintest idea of what he is thinking, or what he imagines he is seeing on that black imageless screen. I am worried about him, and I think I have every reason to be. I never know what tack to take with him, because every time I try to talk to him, his answers show he really isn't paying attention. If he doesn't care for the topic of conversation, he gets nervous and shuts himself up in his room, and I don't see him again until morning when he leaves for school.

I have spoken to his friends' parents and it seems to me that they find themselves in the same situation, more or

LUIGI MALERBA *is the pseudonym of Luigi Bonardi, who was born near Parma in 1927 but has long lived in Rome. His writing includes novels, stories, and children's literature. Malerba tends to experiment with narrative forms, mixing realism and fantasy, irony and philosophical speculation. His darkly humorous novel* The Serpent *(1966) has been translated into English.*

less, with their children. There is the same incomprehension, the same detachment and indifference that exist between me and my son. I don't understand what these kids have in their heads. I have even tried to eavesdrop on them when they are together, and I have discovered that they use a lot of obscenities, but I haven't heard a real, coherent conversation from them. In a word, they can't even talk among themselves.

I am worried, above all, about the void in which they live. I am worried that my son looks at the blank television, that he has no dialogue with anyone; I am worried about his lack of interests and enthusiasm, his silences. He doesn't read newspapers, doesn't go to the movies, doesn't go dancing. I was very different when I was young, but of course today everything has changed. Someone suggested that I try slapping him, but I am opposed to corporal punishment; I am a modern parent and I don't feel I should hit my son because he looks at the blank television or because there is no dialogue between us. This is not to mention that he is already over a foot taller than I am, and I wouldn't want to give him the idea of putting his hands on me—one never knows.

It was just a little while ago that I told him, Find yourself a hobby, something to amuse you, or a game, like tennis or football or pole vaulting—in short, a diverting sport that will be good for your health. I would even rather see him shooting pool than doing nothing, but he started laughing when I mentioned it, as if I had said something strange and ridiculous. If you don't like shooting pool, why not try bowling, skateboarding, frisbee? In this way I showed him that I am more up-to-date than he thinks and it really isn't a laughing matter. I know that when a boy takes a liking to a game, even if he neglects school, at least his mind is occupied with something and he isn't running worse risks. I am thinking of drugs, naturally. Today drugs are the nightmare of all parents, just as venereal disease once was. Syphilis can now be cured, but it seems that nothing can be done about that plague, drugs.

A month has passed since my son asked me to buy him a motorcycle, a Lambretta. At first I was surprised, but I said to myself, Better the Lambretta than drugs. I asked him a few questions about it, cautiously, to avoid irritating him. I recalled that some years ago a cousin of mine had bought a motorcycle for his son, who later took off and was never seen again. Every so often he sends a postcard—from Baden-Baden, Hamburg, Marseilles, Amsterdam—and everything ends there. All those years of affection down the drain. A month ago a card arrived from Helsinki. What can he be doing in Helsinki? I wouldn't want anything like this to happen to my son, I said to myself, and so I bought him a used Lambretta, with a rather run-down engine that hadn't been properly overhauled. He can't get very far on this, I thought.

But he didn't have the slightest intention of running away from home. In fact, ever since I bought him the motorcycle, you could say that he has overcome his disgust for talking to me, and once in a while he addresses a few words in my direction. He has even explained why he needed the Lambretta—he told me that he uses it in a game he plays with his friend. Thank goodness, I said to myself; if he has finally taken a liking to a game, he will calm down. Maybe he will change this negative attitude, maybe he will be more serene, maybe he will eventually let me in on his secrets, as fathers and sons used to do with one another.

One night he came home all sweaty with a rip in his jacket. He sat down in front of me and said that he had had so much fun he thought he would go out of his mind. Thus I came to know what his game consists of. He explained to me that it requires two players: one drives the Lambretta; the other directs the game. They drive down the narrow streets near the Campo dei Fiori where there are never any police, and they snatch the handbags of women who walk through the neighborhood. In the beginning, they got some practice by stealing bags from old ladies who couldn't run, and hence the risk was reduced to a minimum. After a month of practice, they pounced on the tourists, preferably foreign tourists.

I asked him what they did with the handbags and he explained that they return them by mail when they find an address among the papers; otherwise they throw them in the Tiber. He says they have mailed one to the United States, to Minneapolis, and others to Canada, Brazil, even Australia and Japan. And the money, what did they do with the money? We keep that, he answered; if we didn't, the game would lose all its meaning and we wouldn't be amused anymore. Besides, the money pays for expenses— gas for the Lambretta, repairs, the postage needed to send the handbags to their rightful owners, and so on. Keep in mind, he added, that we often find foreign currency, and we lose a lot with black-market exchanges.

The women whose bags are stolen often start screaming and chasing after us, my son told me, and this is very exciting. When we finally reach a safe place far away from the victim, we usually burst out laughing and then we go to a pizzeria or the movies. My friend and I always divide the money in half; we divide the expenses in half too. We take turns driving, and the one who sits behind the driver must choose the victim and snatch her handbag; this is the rule of the game. In a word, it seems they're having a fine time—lucky them.

Ever since my son started playing the purse-snatching game, he has improved a great deal. In the morning he goes to school, returns home at 1:30, does his homework, and then goes out with the Lambretta. Sometimes he brings his friend home with him and they do their homework together before going out. At other times it is my son who goes to his friend's house, especially when they have homework in mathematics, because the boy's father is an engineer and he helps them do the equivalences and equations and solve the word problems. I myself don't understand mathematics, but I gladly listen to the poetry they must learn by heart—Pascoli's "Valentino" ("Oh! Valentino, new-clothed like the hawthorn buds!"), D'Annunzio's "Shepherds of Abruzzo" ("September is here. Let's move on; it's time to migrate"), Leopardi's "The Infinite" ("This solitary hill was always dear to me")—all very beautiful poems. I have always liked poetry and I remember much of it from my own school days, so I can help them recite without even looking at the book.

My son often comes home very late at night, when I am already in bed, but if he returns early, we sit in front of the television and watch a program together, and when it's over, we exchange our opinions about it. The times when he sat for hours before the blank screen are long gone. If there is nothing interesting on television, he tells me about the purse-snatching game, always with great enthusiasm. One night he told me he and his friend had managed to snatch five bags. Every so often I give him some advice because I am always afraid that during their getaways down those congested little streets, they might fall or collide with someone. I made him promise me that they will pay the insurance with the next snatch. They told me they don't have any other plans for it. They are splendid boys. Give them a little time, and they'll even be as happy and carefree as they should be at their age.

The other night they came home happier than usual and announced that they had bought a Kawasaki. I had to go down into the courtyard to see it. They told me to calm down—they had already arranged everything, including the insurance and the registration. I myself will never get on a Kawasaki, but I must admit that it is undoubtedly a beautiful object.

(1979)

The Other Family

Dacia Maraini

PIETRO AND PAOLO WAKE ME in the morning by jumping on my chest. Feeling suffocated, I open my eyes. Pietro is sitting astride my belly, bouncing up and down as if he were riding a jackass; Paolo is kneeling on my legs, laughing.

"Mamma, it's time to get up."

"What time is it?"

"Six."

"Can't I sleep a little more?"

"No, you have to help us get dressed and then make breakfast. Get up."

"But what time is it?"

"Seven."

Poet, novelist, and playwright DACIA MARAINI *was born in Florence in 1936 and currently lives in Rome. An important figure in the Italian feminist movement, she has long dedicated her writing to the exploration of social and political issues. Her often translated work includes the fact-based thriller,* Isolina *(1985), and the historical novel,* The Silent Duchess *(1990), winner of the distinguished Campiello Prize. In this story, she presents a wife and mother who is the main breadwinner, although with a surprising twist.*

"What a liar. You're saying anything just to make me get up: what a liar! Let me sleep a little more."

"Mamma wants to sleep, Pietro. Get off her."

I turn over and try to go back to sleep. But my two sons' silence makes me suspicious. I turn my head and, sure enough, find them in the center of the room with paper and matches, absorbed in lighting a fire.

I leap up, slap both their faces, slip back into bed. But at this point I can't sleep anymore. I remain horizontal a few more minutes, arms crossed behind my head, eyes half closed, trying to get used to the light entering the open window. Then I get up and start the day.

I go the kitchen to make breakfast for the boys and Giorgio. At eight o'clock we're all sitting around the table. Pietro is trying to persuade his older brother to play with him: he's filling his mouth with milk and squirting it on Paolo's back.

"Tell your son to stop it."

"Stop it, Pietro."

"Paolo's doing it too."

"Both of you stop it."

"Tell your son to stop it."

"I've told him."

"Give him a smack."

Pietro takes off before I make it in time to grab him. And when I get close, running behind him, he squirts a mouthful of warm milk in my face.

"Hit him!"

"Why don't *you* hit him?"

"You know I'm against violence. Your son is such an imbecile."

"He's your son too."

"He's my son too, but he resembles you. Paolo is more like me. In fact, if it weren't for Pietro, he'd be different: he'd be very good."

"It's late now, boys, you have to leave. Where are your schoolbags?"

"Mine is broken."

"What do you mean 'broken'? Where did you put it?"

"I threw it away. It was all broken."

"How could you have broken a wooden briefcase?"

"Pietro played football with it."

"Talk to your son," shouts my husband. "He's worse than an imbecile; he's a delinquent."

"It was Paolo, I swear."

"No, it was you."

"Tell him that besides being a delinquent, he's a liar too. But do you smack him? . . . No."

"I've already smacked him."

"Do it again."

"I can't spend all day smacking Pietro."

"I'm against violence, but with that idiot it's necessary."

I chase Pietro through the house while Paolo and his father sit watching with huge bowls of milk in their hands, their hair combed, their eyes serious yet astonished.

I finally manage to put the boys on the elevator. I close the door and return to the house. Giorgio is also getting ready to leave.

"When do you go to Milan?" he asks me.

"Tomorrow."

"This job of yours—a few days here, a few days in Milan—it makes me nervous."

"Why?"

"Because I can't get used to it. Sometimes I think, We're on our own today because Elda has left. Then I come home and find you playing with the kids. Other times I think, I'll go home now and tell Elda the joke that Strapparelli whispered in my ear. But when I open the door, I smell something burning and suddenly remember you've left, and at once I realize Pietro is playing with matches, as he usually is."

"This is my job. What can I do if it forces me to travel back and forth between Milan and Rome?"

"You could find another job."

"I don't think so. I earn a good living with the one I've got. You know your salary isn't enough."

"But at least you could travel on the same days so I wouldn't always be wrong."

"I can't. It depends on the work, not me."

"Sometimes I think you've got someone waiting for you in Milan."

"And who might that be?"

"Another man."

"What rubbish!"

Giorgio smiles with satisfaction. He bends to kiss me on the cheek, fingers his tie into place, and leaves.

I give the maid a few instructions for lunch and then shut myself in the study to work. I prepare my reports, pour over new cases, write. My head is utterly empty. I work mechanically, almost unconsciously.

At one o'clock the door is violently flung open. Pietro runs in, gives me a hug, and kisses me, gluing his sticky lips to my face. He's been eating ice cream.

"How was school?"

"Good. I didn't go."

"What do you mean you didn't go? What about Paolo?"

"Paolo came with me. We went to play football."

"What am I going to do with you? Tell me."

"I'm an imbecile, I know. But where's papa? Please don't tell him."

"I'm not going to tell him, but I'm still going to smack you."

"When do you leave for Milan, mamma?"

"Tomorrow."

"Take me with you?"

"No."

"Why not?"

"Because you know I have things to do."

"But I'd be good and wait for you at the hotel."

"I said no, and not another word about it."

At the table Pietro and Paolo wolf down their lunch in silence, then dash off to play on the terrace. Giorgio reads the newspaper. As soon as he's finished, we both lie down on the bed to rest.

At four o'clock Giorgio leaves again. Pietro and Paolo go to the gardens with their friends. Around seven thirty they return to do their homework, but it's too late and they're tired. After sitting at the table for ten minutes, they fall asleep on their books. I spend the evening doing their homework for them.

"Pietro is corrupting Paolo. They're going to become two good-for-nothings, two delinquents. It'll be your fault."

"Why mine?"

"Because you're not raising them the right way."

"And what about you?"

"I already have enough to do, teaching forty kids at school. When I come home, I'm tired. You know what I always say—we should never have had children; we aren't suited to having a large family."

"Perhaps you're right. We should've just stayed a couple, on our own. But then again perhaps we would've separated by now."

"Why?"

"Because living as a couple is very boring. At a certain point, you don't know what to say anymore."

"You always say the most unpleasant things. Why don't we go to the cinema tonight?"

"I can't. I'm dead tired. You go."

"No, not without you."

"Then let's go to bed."

The next morning I am awakened at the usual hour by Pietro, who straddles my chest and bounces up and down as if I were a donkey.

"What time is it?"

"Five thirty."

"Get my suitcase down from the wardrobe, Pietro."

"Paolo'll get it. I'm busy now."

"Get off; you're hurting me."

"No. A horse can't tell his rider to get off. Shut your eyes and gallop. I want to go to Milan."

"Get off or I'll make you fall."

I get together my bag, my briefcase with the law suit I have to argue, my purse, and my overcoat, and then I leave. Pietro escorts me down to the taxi; Paolo stays with his father, and both of them look out the window to wave goodbye to me.

During the flight I sleep. It's the only time when I feel completely at ease. The noise is deafening, and the gentle movement of the plane rocks me. I awake just before we land. I open my eyes as the plane descends from the clean, luminous blue at four thousand meters to the variegated band of opaque mists and bright white clouds that covers Lombardy.

They recognize me now at the airport: as soon as I arrive, I enter the bar, set my suitcase on the floor, have a coffee, then buy a phone card and call home.

"Is that you, Carlo?"

"When did you arrive?"

"Just now."

"Have a good trip?"

"Yes, I slept."

"I'll come pick you up."

"There's no need; I can easily get a taxi."

When I open the front door, I find Gaspare and Melchiorre on their feet, waiting for me. They are well dressed, well groomed, respectful, and accommodating.

"How are you two?"

"Gaspare received some good marks at school."

"So did Melchiorre."

"And papa?"

"He's doing well. He just left to go to Mass."

"What a pious and orderly family I have."

"Do you want to eat something, mamma?"

"No, I must dash to the office. I'll see you at lunchtime."

The work that has accumulated in the Milan office is

always more than I anticipate, and I wind up returning home late. When I enter, I find the table set and my sons and husband seated, waiting for me.

"You shouldn't have waited. You should have begun."

"We wanted to eat with you."

"Did you have a lot to do?"

"Yes, quite a lot. I'm very tired."

"The plane is tiring."

"Yes, the plane is tiring."

"And packing up is tiring."

"Yes, packing up is tiring."

"And waking early in the morning is tiring."

"Yes, waking early in the morning is tiring."

"How did things go in Rome?"

"Fine."

"Rome is such an annoying city."

"Yes, it's such an annoying city."

"There are so many useless traffic lights."

"It's true; there are so many useless traffic lights."

"And then people there haven't the slightest desire to do anything."

"People there haven't the slightest desire to do anything."

"We Milanesi are the ones who support the peninsula."

"Which peninsula?"

"Italy, no?"

"Ah, Italy."

"Gaspare, Melchiorre, go do your homework."

"Yes, papa. Later, mamma."

"They're becoming two hypocrites."

"Who?"

"Your two sons."

"They're yours as well."

"They're mine as well, but they resemble you. Silent and hypocritical. They pretend to be angels. But they're up to no good. They've already learned how to play their parts to perfection. They don't give a damn about me."

"What's so terrible about them?"

"They're fakes, I'm telling you, fakes and liars."

"So, have you finished your book?"

"No, darling. But I'm at a good point. Only eight chapters to go."

"What's the story? You've never told me."

"It's about a man who leads two lives."

"Interesting. But why don't you hurry up and get it done? You've been dragging on this book for many years."

"Because I have to think about it. Besides, the more I think about it, the more complicated it becomes. Do you think a man can have, not two women at the same time, but two families?"

"I think so."

"Do you think it's moral?"

"No."

"Well, this is the problem that interests me: how to reconcile morality with what is more vital and more deeply felt in us—sex, the need for independence, the taste for the abnormal."

"Will you finish it this year?"

"Yes, of course. Even if I don't work much on it, I still work."

"And who'll publish it for you?"

"I don't know. I'll find a publisher, I imagine. But it's going to be very difficult."

In the afternoon I take my two sons to the cinema while my husband stays at home to work. When we return, we find him sitting in the entrance hall, playing with the cat. We ask him if he's worked. He answers yes. Gaspare and Melchiorre smile incredulously.

At eighty thirty we sit down to supper. I feel so tired that I have no appetite. The boys tell me boring stories. Then we all sit in front of the television and don't move till eleven o'clock. I'm unable to follow the programs because I keep dropping off to sleep, my eyelids burn, I stare blindly. Gaspare and Melchiorre wake me every so often with their shrill laughter.

"When do you leave for Rome, mamma?"

"Thursday."

"Then this time you're staying four days with us."

"Yes, four days."

"When are you going to take me to Rome, mamma?"

"Never."

"I'd like to go to Rome with you, to see if it's really as ugly and dirty as papa says."

At eleven the two boys go to bed, and in the dark room, lit by the pale blue television screen, Carlo and I sit alone.

"Listen—tell me if you like this opening."

"What are you talking about?"

"My novel, darling."

"Ah, yes. How does it begin?"

"This is the beginning of chapter ten: 'On a warm, breezy summer evening when the oak leaves were trembling slightly, filling the air with a green shudder . . .' Do you like it?"

"Isn't this sentence a little too long?"

"Not at all. Listen again: 'On a warm, breezy summer evening when the oak leaves I glimpsed from the window at the farthest end of my room were trembling lightly, filling the air with a burning shudder . . .' Which do you think is better? 'Burning' or 'green'?"

"I don't know."

"'On a warm, breezy summer evening when . . .' Listen to how good it sounds: it's a wave that advances slow and powerful—you hear it arrive and wait for it to break, you wait while holding your breath. Isn't that right?"

"How does it continue?"

"'On a warm, breezy summer evening . . .' Perhaps in place of 'warm' I should put 'hot.' What do you say? It gives more of a muggy feel. Because it needs mugginess. Meanwhile the wave advances. You hear it arrive. Here it is . . . 'when the oak leaves were trembling lightly, filling the air around me . . .' I want to add 'around me.' This works better; doesn't it seem so to you? So 'around me with a shudder'—what did I say before?"

"Let's go to bed."

"You go; I'm going to keep on working."

"What do you have to do?"

"I have to find the right phrase. It's very important to find the right phrase."

"I don't think you'll ever publish this book."

"Why?"

"Because you don't want to. How did you get the idea about two lives?"

"When I was a lad, I loved two girls at the same time. But I would feel so bad about it. I felt guilty."

"How did it turn out?"

"Badly. You can't parcel out yourself for very long. You get sick."

The next day I resume the usual Milanese life. Gaspare and Melchiorre go to school, I go to the office, Carlo shuts himself in the study to write his novel. At one o'clock we eat lunch together. In the afternoon I return to work, Carlo plays with the cat, and the two boys do their homework. Sometimes, around seven, we go to the cinema, or else we spend the evening before the television.

A couple days later I pack my bags, fill my briefcase with the suits I have to study, with letters and accounts, and then make my way back to Rome. Carlo accompanies me to the airport.

"Ciao. Try to finish your novel."

"I work hard on it, you know. I expect to finish it within the year. Then it'll be me who supports you. I'll let you live like a lady of leisure."

As soon as I arrive in Rome, I buy a phone card, head for the nearest phone, and call home.

"Is that you, mamma?"

"I've just arrived."

"Do you know Pietro set papa's study on fire?"

"And what did he do to him?"

"Nothing. He's waiting for you to come back to punish him. He said he wants you to hit him with the belt from your dress."

(1968)

Honeymoon in Naples

Corrado Alvaro

I WENT BACK HOME after many years, and as I drew near my town, details from my childhood were suddenly brought back to mind. I even remembered the holes in the walls, those holes where the stone is worn away by wind and southern sun, where swallows build their nests, where, to fend off bad luck, women hide children's teeth and hair fallen from combs, and where I used to hide nails and buttons and whatever else I found in the rain-swept streets (my cache, in short), where sometimes summer brought forth a pale, slender shoot of wheat from soil gathered by the wind (it was also my garden). So many such things I remembered. Yet as soon as I entered the house, I was met by the most vivid memory of all: the chest of drawers in my father's room, the chest whose wide drawer sometimes stretched over my child's head like a baldacchino. There

CORRADO ALVARO *(1895–1956) was born in the Calabrian village of San Luca and, despite personal attacks by the Fascists, pursued a career as a journalist. His fiction and essays focus on the plight of southern rural workers confronted by exploitive conditions. A characteristic work is his novel* Revolt in Aspromonte *(1930).*

my father would store mysterious things. In my eyes, this piece of furniture with its black columnlike molding still represented what it had seemed to me long ago: the temple of dreams. And I remembered that a wasp had made its nest in the wood, in a hole, with a soft blond dust. I expected that my father might by chance open the drawers and let me look inside, now that I was taller. The same smell of the past whirled around me, and the resin from the wood, distilled unnoticed one summer, bore an intoxicating smell for me.

"This is my mamma's dress, her honeymoon dress. And these are her boots."

I felt the silk of that dress beneath my fingers. It was called faille then, as I had heard my mother say, a light brown silk with the scent of faded flowers. It hissed under my hands. The high collar, the puff sleeves, the charming strip of lace on the bodice. And the tall yellow shoes, the soles scarcely scuffed, the insteps scarcely wrinkled, on that too-brief stroll through the streets of Naples.

They had gone to Naples for their honeymoon. No sooner had my grandfather given his daughter to that thirty-year-old man than he was filled with regret. When the wedding dinner ended, he shut himself up in his room, completely flustered, and refused to bid them farewell. "Scoundrel!" he said. My grandmother, barefoot, started sighing in the kitchen near the dying fire. The bride's sisters remained silent, sitting in the corner like bundles of laundry. The bride in her rustling dress, wearing her little straw hat on her front of her head, disappeared on her horse down the road to the sea. Beside her was my father's shadow, along the parched streams where the water surprised by summer shone stagnant in the sunlight.

The bridegroom had the same big wallet that I saw as a child. He kept it jealously buttoned in a pocket that he had also fastened with a pin. On the train he never closed his eyes. Every so often he would place a hand on the suitcase to reassure himself that it was there. He scrutinized anyone who boarded and anyone who got off. The bride was happy to be sitting next to a trustworthy man in a world so huge where the Lord had not created even two faces that resembled each other. Her straw hat with the delicate buttercups, which lay on the luggage rack, bobbed in her mind. The huge world, speaking in the voices of the train and the dawn, took notice of them and clasped them close together. She was happy to have taken a man she knew, who spoke her own dialect, a friend. They looked round for the most humble figure, and their eyes lit on a woman dressed in black with a child. They clung to her as to a messenger from Providence. "Has his father passed away?" asked the bride, gazing at the little one. Thus began their conversation. She had guessed. She shook her head, pitied him, and asked about his father with a venerable decency even while speaking of a man who was no longer alive. Then they fell silent because they had nothing to say, except to point out the gardens along the railway. Still, they regarded one another as friends, because pain readily joins simple folk.

They reached Naples near evening. The broad streets frightened them. Everyone had something to say to them: the coachmen, the children, and certain people who would suddenly step away from the walls to suggest the address of a furnished room in a respectable house. The bride-groom had unbuttoned his jacket and was using two hands to carry the heavy suitcase against his belly, in such a way that he could feel the hard corner of the wallet with his thumb. She had tried to respond like a Christian by saying no to every question that the unknown people had asked. But the bridegroom warned her with his eyes and walked straight ahead as if they had not spoken to him. She was afraid. She clung to his arm and let herself trail behind, weary of the too-hard pavement, made entirely of stone like the floor in the church at her village. The houses greeted them with dizzying balconies on high floors, with secret windows that struck them with a panic they had never experienced. She admired her man who was so familiar with life, who walked straight ahead, courageous. She would strive to be worthy of him.

"We won't go to a hotel," said the bridegroom. "Those swindlers won't get our money." He had already made this remark before their departure, and he seemed to have devised a plan to deceive an entire city that was danger-ously lying in wait for him. They were heartened by the movement of people wearing dark colors—old men, their wives, and children at their sides. But what were all those people doing, pouring through street, stopping hesitantly, looking round, moving down the long sidewalks and then pausing at a street corner as if expecting someone? Were they expecting them? The bridegroom would have taken his wife to a safe place, the home of certain people he had known ten years before, when he was a soldier. He would have requested a room for a few days, and they would have been out of harm's way. But the city seemed changed to him, and he couldn't get his bearings. They stopped in an immense piazza, their eyes fixed on a clock that was suddenly illuminated while the sun was still shining. The shops sparkled like chapels, and the owners sat at their doors. The couple stood watching the people pass by, searching for someone to ask about the street they were seeking. They did not want to confide in the first passerby. Humanity wore faces never seen before, the faces of occupations and passions that they did not recognize, that filled them with foreboding. Finally they found a man who resembled the people in their village. They confided their questions to him in a low voice, observed all his actions, heard his response and his directions, but hesitated before moving and watched him as he drew away.

The house they were seeking was located in a seedy working-class street where they arrived amid the uproar of voices and carts, amid the din of merchants, amid silent crowds milling around pawnshops. Here they took heart again and felt as if they were in their village. The wretched little women crossing the street, the cripples who came forth here and there like signs of destiny, the fat bejeweled landladies who made everybody's hair stand on end, the children playing on the sidewalks, the vendors who boasted shrilly about their goods unashamed to shout so loudly— all this put them in good humor. They felt they were among friends. Then the bridegroom had the bride admire the abundance of fruit and goods displayed on the street without fear of thieves. He said to amaze her, "Just imagine how you can find grapes here in every season, along with any kind of fruit any time."

They found the house they were seeking. He rushed

inside, shouting with the joy he used to feel in the good days, ten years before, trying to revive the same intonation in his voice, the same words of greeting. But he encountered an old woman who could scarcely recognize him. She rummaged through her memory, then emitted a wan "Ah yes, yes!" and stood gazing at him. Her husband had died; her sons had each taken a job and married. Even her daughter had married, and in saying this she looked at him. The bride lowered her eyes, blushing. But the bridegroom filled the moment of silence with his most piercing, most joyful voice, that voice of the past. "We've come to Naples and we thought of you. You're still beautiful, still young." He also said other things to which she listened with a faint smile. She opened the room she had shared with her husband, wallpapered in red with an old faded floral design, furnished with a huge bed and photo enlargements veiled in black to fend off sorrow and flies. She brought an oil lamp and took the two lire on which they had agreed as compensation.

The city outside shook the window panes with its tremor. The bridegroom bolted the door and leaned a chair against it. The bride sat on a chair placed next to a chest of drawers where a small statue of the Madonna in a bell jar wore a frayed blue dress and a tilted crown. She listened to the wheeze of the oil lamp. When her husband was seated at the table, solitude fell upon them. Then the bridegroom said in a low voice, "Now we shall eat. I've thought of everything." He opened the suitcase and took out a parcel. Another parcel he set aside, saying, "This is for tomorrow."

They had not said it to one another but it crossed both their minds: they must think about those who would come later, the children. The bride kept her hands in her lap, hands accustomed to work and now for the first time idle and embarrassed to be idle. The bridegroom cut up the chicken that he had laid on a piece of newspaper. He poured the wine and looked at it against the lamp. Meanwhile, trying to laugh, he said in a low voice, "Come sit at the table. Let's eat our food, from our village. They don't have this food here. I bet if the mistress saw it, she'd ask us for a bit. See how well we're doing? We're not spending our money in hotels. Instead, tomorrow we'll buy an embroidered cradle in pink. Pink or blue?"

My mother rested her arm on the table and wept silently.

(1929)

The American Woman

Domenico Rea

I WAS AT HOME, ALONE. To ease the discomfort of the sirocco, I had decided to sit out on the terrace. Next to the chaise longue I had set a bottle of dry white wine, very cold, and every so often I lifted a glass to my lips. I needed to raise the pressure.

The experiment was yielding results. Or perhaps my spirit had been quickened by the white fringe of the broad blue awning, the blaze of bougainvillea and pinkish ivy intertwined on the railing, and the incredible color of the sea, uniform and intense, amid the swarm of ships, sail boats, and steamers ferrying back and forth from Ischia and Capri. I hadn't the slightest desire for anything, and my only expense of effort was to empty my mind. True, a

---

Born in Nocera near Salerno, DOMENICO REA *(1921–1994) lived in Naples. His realistic novels and stories sensitively chronicle Neapolitan life after World War II, with particular attention to the poor and the working class. His novel* A Blush of Shame *(1959) was translated, but his work remains largely unfamiliar to English-language readers. This story about a brief encounter between an Italian man and an American woman addresses the cultural stereotypes that developed as the tourist industry rapidly expanded in the 1960s.*

book with large type (an adventure-filled history written by an early traveler in the wake of the Colombian explorations) lay open on my knees. Yet only now and then did I cast a glance to read a few phrases, much as I lifted the wine to my mouth.

The sirocco is one of nature's fevers, low-grade but persistent. It weighs down the body, spreads a veil of idiocy over the intellect. The sea benefits: it is stripped bare, displaying colors that it would scarcely reveal in different weather. Abandoned to the pleasure of indolence, I experienced the sudden ringing of the telephone as a physical assault. It was afternoon, and I couldn't imagine who it might be, who would dare phone. The people with whom I had business dealings would be resting at that inane hour. My relatives were at beaches and seaside resorts along the Amalfi coast. I let the phone scream and was pleased to chalk up a victory over curiosity when I noticed that my body remained motionless, without a start.

But this lasted too briefly. The phone resumed ringing, impersonal and violent, and with no other intention but to silence it, I padded barefoot across the quiet coolness of the living room and picked up.

"Who is it?" I said with annoyance. A barely intelligible voice responded. "Who are you?" I shouted. The voice on the other end seemed cowed by my tone. Only when I expressed myself more politely did I manage to grasp that the person who sought me was a foreign woman passing through Naples. "Ah," I said, "and what do you want?" From her disastrous Italian I gathered that she was translating one of my scientific articles on the behavior of coleoptera and wished to ask me some questions.

"When do you leave?" I asked, weighing my options.
"Tomorrow morning."

"How shall we handle it?" I asked. I had no desire to
dress and go out at that hour, nor did I care to meet an
American woman. If she had been young, the meeting
could have held a certain interest. But judging from her
halting, guttural tone, I imagined her to be elderly, with the
hard features and fussiness of another American woman I
had known years ago—a crushing disappointment in my
salad days. Upon being invited to Rome by an American
lady who had expressed interest in my work, I was filled
with fond hopes. A friend assured me that I might spend
some special evenings with the beautiful American who,
in sending her invitations by telegram and express mail as
if her life depended on our meeting, had underscored her
desire to become acquainted with the author himself. She
had to be traveling alone and, perhaps recalling the photo
of me that appeared in several American magazines, she
longed to combine utility with delight, pursuing the true
reason for her fascination through the usual conversations,
at once serious and pointless. American women are no
different from other women. Yet they don't all wear glasses,
possess enough facial hair to qualify as bearded, and come
shriveled with age, like my translator. She talked constantly
about herself and America, about the dreadful state of the
sciences in Italy, about the need to make work—performed
with perseverance and fastidiousness—the only goal of her
life.

The legacy of that memory was so much alive that, for
an instant, facing the possibility of another encounter, I
feared my translator might be the same old woman, obliv-

ious of the fact that she had already met me. I was mistaken. This was undoubtedly a different woman. I hadn't the faintest idea of how I might ascertain whether she was young or old, tall or short, beautiful or ugly. So I began to ask questions like "What brought you to Naples? When did you arrive? Are you on your own?" I gathered that she had taken advantage of a chance car trip, motivated by curiosity to visit a city about which she had heard a great deal, both in Italy and in the United States. At this point, she was disappointed to find herself wandering around alone and so, recalling that I was based here, she phoned me, of course intending to ask the questions about coleoptera as well. If I cared to serve as her guide for a little while, she would be immensely grateful for my attentiveness.

The detail about the car trip led me to think, at least for a moment, that I was dealing with a young woman. But I immediately remembered that the first American woman, although old, had had agility and vitality to spare. Another detail struck me as more interesting: her desire to see my city and her chance arrival by hitchhiking. This was very American, relying largely on whim and the instinct to change one's situation and place, behavior that reflects the psychology of a once-nomadic people. Yet beyond these impressions lay something obscurely charming which, despite my unwillingness, pushed me to say:

"Fine. Give me half an hour, and I shall meet you." She must have smiled and brightened up because her "Sì, grazie" hit me like a flash of light.

"Where are you now? . . . How did you get there?" I asked again. "Try to find the main entrance to the Palazzo

Reale, an easily recognizable spot that everyone knows, and I will be there as soon as I can." With this understanding, I hung up the phone and slowly returned to the terrace.

Either something in the landscape had changed, or I had changed and perceived it from another perspective. The sirocco must have passed because the sea appeared wrinkled to me, curved like a sphere, with the sails like so many triangular bits of white paper. It was a toy sea, invented by a child, and since I was engaged in a secret dialogue with him, a shiver ran down my back, a familiar signal that announced a renewed interest in life. I took another sip of wine, picked up the ice bucket, and entered the house, immediately seized by doubt as to how I should dress, whether in linen or wool, in a light or dark color, as a respectable scholar or some blasé fellow. In the interval I remembered that I had made a tentative appointment with a friend for that evening, desirous as I was to meet his very attractive cousin, and this detail, this possible means of escape, drove me to a positive decision. I would speak first with the American woman and, without returning home, would head to my friend's. I decided to wear a dark suit. Just as I was on the verge of leaving, I phoned my friend to tell him that I would definitely spend the evening with him and his cousin and that in fact I expected to arrive early.

In the mirror I noticed that the navy wool suit fit me perfectly. It made me appear thinner and younger than I really was. My agreeable self-image gave me a feeling of elation. I took pleasure in moving, speaking, acting, loving things and people, and, when I descended the stairs on my way out, seeing Vesuvius loom before me and then the scattered mosaic of coastal buildings on the Sorrentine peninsula, I found myself walking with the light step of a dancing faun. Besides, from the Straits of Capri there appeared the white profile of an ocean liner, symbol of good tidings, of a particular disposition of fate. All these signs, exterior as well as interior, inclined me to feel brilliant, to overestimate even the sordid aspects of reality, and, after speeding through Naples as if through the streets of an equatorial city, one eye fixed on the sight of the advancing ship, I arrived at the entrance of the Palazzo Reale. It was empty.

I didn't even have time to repress my incipient frustration because at once the uniformed doorman was careful to tell me:

"A signorina has just come to look for you, Professore. She slipped into the palazzo . . . heading in that direction."

"What does she look like?" I asked. He made a roguish gesture, screwing the index finger of his left hand into his cheek. I gunned the car into the first courtyard. She wasn't there. I proceeded to the second—nothing. "How crazy these Yankees are!" I thought. But as I pulled into the third courtyard, my eyes feasted on a marvelous figure. The woman had her back to me; she was gazing up at the seventeenth-century windows and the roof garden. I slowly approached in the car, stopped, got out, and went to meet her, saying in Italian:

"Excuse me, are you Signora Natalie Norwar?"

"Yes," she answered in English.

"I am the man you phoned," I said in Italian, and she followed suit.

"Was it really you?" she asked, surprised.

"Yes."

She burst into laughter, all'americana, saying:

"You're so young. I thought you were a distinguished elderly gentleman."

We shared the laugh. Her gaze returned to the garden, and I asked:

"Does this palazzo please you?"

"It's like a fairy tale."

"The kings in the good old days weren't foolish. They reserved the alleys for the people, and for themselves the staircases, drawing rooms, and gardens."

We laughed again.

"Have you been walking for very long? . . . You're tired. Climb in; we'll drive."

"Your car is very handsome," she said. "I'm happy to be here."

"In the car?" I asked.

"The whole thing."

We drove off, and as we left through the main entrance, I was pleased to receive a bow from the tall, lordly concierge, who had once served as the Crown Prince's chief groom.

"Do you know who told me about you?"

"Who?" I asked, truly surprised, even a bit suspicious.

She mentioned a woman's name, a terrible name, the worst gossip in Rome. This woman had once been my friend. She now believed herself to be the beneficiary of the most glaring flaws in my southern character.

"But she hadn't told me you would be so young, not a word about it. She did say you're very lighthearted, very . . ."—here she laughed again, all'americana, her eyes vanishing in the creases of her face and eyelids—"very cocksure!" I said, completing her sentence.

The vivaciousness that distinguished this lovely creature, thrown into my path by chance, was suddenly transformed into mistrust. She must have belonged to that category of Americans who wander through the capitals of Europe, welcomed in circles that thrive on gossip. The name of our common friend would have made any man apprehensive. As I drove off to give her a quick glimpse of some working-class quarters of Naples, I asked her:

"And so what questions would you like me to clarify for you?"

I moved far to the left, toward the car door, so that between us there emerged an empty space that could not occasion any misunderstandings.

"How can I help you?"

Her only response was to ask me:

"Do you have a wife?"

"Yes."

"What a shame."

"Why?" I asked.

"It's always a shame to have a wife or husband."

"And you? Do you have a husband?"

"Yes," she answered in English, then reverted to Italian. "I'm divorced."

"Why?"

"It's impossible to explain."

"And now you're free?"

"Yes." She spoke in English again, but quickly shifted

to Italian. "There's an Italian man in love with me. I don't much care for him."

"Ah well," I said, but I would have liked to say, "What difference does it make to me?"

The fear that the evening with her would end in disappointment increased my desire for the company of my doctor friend and his cousin. For this reason, I stopped the car at a small piazza and said:

"This piazza is typical of Naples. Here you will find a sampling of many things, horrible as well as beautiful: alleys, ground-floor flats, children running around like chickens, flower-decked balconies, terraces. Once you've seen this, you've seen everything." I would have liked to add what my tone had already conveyed: "Now we can head back and say goodbye." She had, however, gotten out of the car and invited me to do likewise. She wanted me to accompany her on a short walk down an alley, which appeared to be little more than a couple of meters wide.

The sunset cast an intense reddish glow on the windows of the houses and the children's faces. Perhaps because one could see a mile away that my companion was an American, a group of some fifteen children in every shape and size— fat and gaunt, thin and robust, jabbering and shouting, with the voices of birds and comic talking animals—gathered around her, and I too fell within the circle. Natalie was radiant, smiling. She opened her purse to offer some coins. The children's assault turned furious, persistent, insolent, a milling of tiny human bodies punctuated by screams of "me, me." She was taken by surprise, at once astonished and a bit frightened. Amid the touching, jostling, and shoving, she firmly slipped her arm through mine as if seeking refuge with me. I was deeply struck by her gesture, and something happened when our eyes met, something beyond us, nameless, devoid of meaning, but definitely recorded.

Now I knew what I had to do. I turned toward the children and in dialect told them that we didn't have any more money. For proof I upended Natalie's purse. I showed them my empty pockets, and after a few moments we were left in peace. Night was falling. At the foot of the alley it was already dark. Dusk pulsated on the rooftops. And she, still linked to my arm—even though our thighs brushed together—was uttering a stream of words that varied in the quality of their Italian, at times good, at others poor. She was trying to explain to me that Naples possessed the mystery of certain New York streets, while Rome was completely out in the open, exposed like a wound. Here between the darkness of the alley and the soft light of the sky we seemed to be aloft in a balloon.

I liked this woman an awful lot. I could have embraced her and kissed her fleshy lips as if at the height of passion. Yet the doubt that I might be mistaking a familiarity commonly practiced by decent people—unprejudiced by displays of another sort—made me timid once again. We wandered at length through streets broken by flights of stairs. We observed how some of the churches in Naples possess the unassuming entrances of houses, allowing them to be confused with street-level apartments. They have curtains with leather edges, guarded by shouting vagrants who seem to summon the unaware to gaze at the magical, mysterious arts that unfold inside the tent.

We finally reached the place where we had left the car—

the modest piazza, now surmounted by a sky filled with flamelike stars. The scent of the sea conjured up images of beaches and the coast, and I was on the verge of telling her, "We should have supper together," when I noticed that in the car she sat beside me with a relaxed air, soft and yielding. As I turned the key in the ignition, I gave her a look that asked, "What you want to do?" and as if she had understood or I had spoken aloud, she said:

"Why don't we have supper together?"

I agreed and added:

"Thank you. But let's go to a simple, quiet place, away from Naples. We could go to Salerno, to a trattoria that has been handed down from father to son for more than a hundred years."

"Is it far?"

"About sixty kilometers. We can be back by midnight."

She said that this was impossible. She had to return by ten at the latest. Tomorrow she planned to leave early. We compromised—we would return between half past ten and eleven o'clock—but I had to be very insistent to get her to play this game with the half hour. I stopped again to phone my doctor friend and beg his pardon. She remained in the car, utterly motionless, and I could have sworn that she seemed worried. Although she had proposed our supper, she was now having second thoughts. I bought cigarettes and a newspaper, and when I returned, she was gone. I discovered her on the telephone in the bar that was visible through the windshield. Suddenly she hung up.

"Where did you go?" I asked when she returned.

"Oh, over there," she answered, and I understood that she didn't wish me to press her further.

While we sped along the highway as if accompanying the impetuous river of stars that hung over us, Natalie drew away from my side. She retreated into a mindset that did not bode well. In the alley, I would have said, "One need only act," but now I felt that she was far away, possibly troubled. She said:

"Please return on time, whatever it takes."

"If you like," I replied, "if you are so worried about losing sleep, we can forego Salerno. We can have supper together another time."

She was silent, then said:

"Let's go to Salerno, but let's get back on time."

I fell into a black mood, although much against my will. I began to hum a song. I felt that human beings were intentionally unhappy. A little compliance would have been sufficient, and we could have plucked the flower that bloomed by chance and which, for this reason, was much more beautiful than any cultivated flower. Instead she obstinately maintained a silence that bordered on rudeness. Sunk in the seat, her head grazing the bottom edge of the window, she stared at the dark road.

"Look on the right," I said to break the ice. "Don't miss the view of the Gulf of Salerno at night." My gesture of goodwill seemed to please her, so I ventured further: "Why so gloomy? You can confide in me. Does it have to do with that man?"

She allowed thirty seconds to elapse, then said:

"Yes, he has stolen my peace of mind. He abandoned his wife and children for me."

"Do you love him?"

She didn't answer. Then, as if pursuing the secret thread of an obsession, she added:

"He constantly follows me."

"Do you like to see him suffer?"

No answer. Then she said:

"He's insanely jealous."

"Does he know that you've come to Naples?"

Salerno lay at our feet, stretching out its dragon's tail. Just as before in the alley, Natalie was overcome with pleasure and said:

"I'd rather not think about anything anymore."

The trattoria where I took her, Don Peppino's on Vico della Neve, pushed her resolution to an extreme. We toasted our meeting, proposing that we would attend only to our happiness that evening. She found everything good—the Gragnano wine, the pizza and the tripe, the salad of baby snails gratiné. And she drank, drank, drank, so that I couldn't keep up with her. Every so often I glanced at the clock, having decided to keep to our schedule. The image of that man tailing her like a shadow had come between us, pitifully, and in thinking of her misfortune, I grew calm.

I did, however, experience a morbid pleasure in revealing that I was not a tenacious, one-dimensional Casanova, persuaded that relations between man and woman were always the same. My Roman friend's jaw would have dropped if she had seen how I comported myself like an old Neapolitan gentleman, courteous and polite, yet detached. Once in a while, even she took pleasure in playing a similar role.

"We shall get back in time," I said. But I had the impression that Natalie wasn't so worried now. The wine had loosened her tongue, and she spoke of her father, her mother, herself. At fifteen she had broken out in a boil, and her parents (papà was a scientist) made an arrangement with the parents of a neighboring boy who suffered from the same condition whereby they might recover together. The parents then departed, although not without leaving the cure entirely to their children.

She laughed, all'americana. And I laughed with her.

At twenty she married an Oxford biology professor, but after three weeks she had to divorce him because of a delicate matter regarding his bad timing in love. Years later, after the professor had married a friend of Natalie's, he paid her a visit and wished to show her, with his second wife's consent, that his timing had now improved. She laughed again, all'americana. And I laughed with her. She then began to say that I had beautiful hands, beautiful eyes, that our common friend in Rome had never told her I might be "so young," that she had phoned me to free herself. . . .

"From whom?" I asked. She pointed to herself, lifting a finger to her chest. "Are you free now?" In response she whispered a "sì" that was girlish and very sweet.

I couldn't grasp where the little girl ended and the woman began. I tried to make eye contact with her, and when I thought I had established that our instincts were unmistakably in agreement, her gaze exploded, like a shell launched from a mortar, and the agreement was canceled. Nothing in her behavior, considering her education, led one to believe that she might cross the boundaries of merely a pleasant meeting. Yet everything, considering her education from a different point of view, left open the door to hope. Not knowing precisely how to act, I said:

"The hour has arrived. This is the moment to leave if we want to reach Naples in time."

It was a way of laying the facts before her; and she, reverting to the silent, sad frame of mind that had lasted during the journey, urged me to hurry, to pay the bill and leave. Walking without touching, we arrived at the car. She returned to her seat, I to mine. I headed for the road along the sea, and as soon as she saw the water, she begged me to stop. With the motor running, I let her climb out to satisfy this latest americanata of hers, this all-American whim. When she reached the railing at the seafront, she signaled me to join her. I pretended not to understand. She called me, and again I feigned incomprehension. After admiring the coast, she hurried back, saying:

"You naughty man, why didn't you come to see?"

"It doesn't interest me."

With her head on the headrest and her body sunk in the seat, she pulled a long face and repeated the word "naughty" in a terribly drawn-out tone. I then turned and began to kiss the fishlike pout of her lips. She let me kiss her, motionless and unrestrained, and when I moved away, she invited me with a gentle squeeze to repeat the game, so that we kissed two, three, four, five, six, a thousand times until I wound up in her seat and she in mine.

With her arm circling my shoulders, I started the car, saying:

"We're late now." She didn't respond. And so when we reached the junction at Vietri, I said, "There are two roads back. This one runs inland, and within fifty minutes we can be in Naples. That one runs along the coast, the most beautiful coast in the world. Maiori, Amalfi, Praiano, Positano—we call it the Via della Indie, the path of the Indies, and it reaches Naples at dawn. Which do you prefer?"

"Indie," she replied. My car sped off like a white steed into a night strewn with stars, villas perched on cliffs, roads bright as ancient fairy tales. I cared for her, cared very deeply, and she in turn must have seen me as the knight on whom she relied to enter places filled with ogres. We passed by beaches, inlets, the Torre Normanna; we left fishing boats and mysteries behind us, and, after a long ride over the winding paths of the forest, we arrived at Ravello, at a hotel with Gothic windows.

In the morning, she awoke frantic.

"We must return to Naples at once," she said.

"Fine, in a moment . . ."

"No, now, fast."

"Certainly, as soon as I'm dressed."

She was ready to leave, holding her purse. Once again she became hard, obstinate, fierce.

"Faster," she said.

I gave her a hostile glance, and she said:

"I forgot my man at the hotel."

"Which man?"

"Mine."

(1976)

Noontide at Anacapri

Alberto Savinio

THE CAMPANILE OF ANACAPRI has struck noon. The streets lie deserted. Open stand the doors of country houses and villas, whence food cooked at length exhales a warm breath. A propitious hour. It is the great meriggio, friends, the mythical midday. At this hour, the spirits of air, sea, and forest rise and walk abroad. Confident that I shan't be disturbing my little brothers, I pursue the path that leads to Caprile. From the piazza cinctured by the houses' harmonious arches, the meager balconies that scarcely protrude from facades, the trelliswork of their pergolas, and the white terraces gushing with the violet luxuriance of wisteria, I descend the rustic road that commences with an arrow pointing me in the direction of the Migliera.

ALBERTO SAVINIO *was the pseudonym of Andrea de Chirico (1892–1952), who, like his brother Giorgio, worked in different media: painting, literature, and music. Born in Athens, Savinio lived in Paris, Ferrara, and Rome and was associated with the modernist avant-garde. His fiction tends to be surrealistic. Several works are available in English, including* Speaking to Clio *(1940) and* Childhood of Nivasio Dolcemare *(1941). This imaginative travel piece first appeared in the Florentine newspaper* Nazione.

At the outset, the road runs steep, scattered with stones, set between rough-cast farm walls wherein an abandoned pigsty opens its mouth at intervals, filled with warm bestial shade and redolent of wool. Thence one is freed, and the eye discovers the face of Caprile, the farthest constructed and inhabited point of the island, as well as the latest derivative from the fundamental root *capra* (meaning "goat" in Italian).

Hitherto I had been unacquainted with any part of this land but the labyrinthine interior, more homestead than holiday site, rich in rural life, enclosed in narrow, winding roads, sealed in its odors and labors. But suddenly Caprile shows me its face, smiling at the sight of its polite gardens and fields consecrated to bucolic poetry, this hanging countryside propped up all about and protected by the highest cliffs.

I then realize that all Caprile, all the facades of its houses look westward because of a common nostalgia for the sea, which, down below, behind the brilliant green of the gardens, expatiates buoyant and airy like celestial ether.

What diversity of light, atmosphere, mood has transpired since this morning, when up through the stones of Monte Solaro I clambered toward Barbarosa's castle, amidst clouds that surrounded me, obstructing the vista!

Little by little the sky cleared. Now it is limpid. The sun blazes on the fields and gleams on the sea. A momentous hush has fallen. But the hour isn't dead. A mysterious, divine wind, a guest at once nimble and witty, trips through this midday peace and animates everything with cool madness.

How docile Solaro appears, glimpsed from this angle! How calm its face as it overlooks the fertile fields of the plain and the open sea! How charming this mountain is! How moderate! How "Greek"!

Three masses of naked stone shine in the sun beneath long strands of cirrus stirred by the divine wind like sheer veils. These peaks tower over the steep slope softened by shrubbery that is interspersed with countless little rocks like white-crested waves.

The transparency of the air has drawn these three masses so near that if I were scarcely to extend a hand, it would seem easy to touch them. Impelled by the most high and sacred wind, they simultaneously reach toward the open sea, which at this hour is nothing but liquid color, tenuous surface, extremely delicate.

The road is no longer a road but a path. Every road on Capri is thus: infirm of purpose, without resistance, blundering. They abandon you on the most beautiful paths, then perhaps pick up again here and there, intermittent, in fits and starts. Temperamental roads, like Magyar violinists. Indeed, in just a short distance, this one too disappears, and my way is marked only by the edges of the fields, by stones arranged in a row, occasionally dropping off in an abrupt descent like the beds of dry streams.

Nothing troubles the sublime silence but the gentle rustle of fronds, broken by thuds from the hoe of a solitary peasant, whom my eye vainly endeavors to discover amidst the thicket of orange and lemon trees and the dark, leaden foliage of the olives.

A lizard flashes across the path, pauses for an instant, its heart beating in its throat, and stares at me from atop a rock, then darts away, disappearing through a fissure betwixt the stones.

Pointy aloe and prickly pear border the path. But up here their broad, fleshy leaves are not marred by the eulogizing effusions of visitors all atwitter. The wave of tourism does not spread so far. Seldom are foreigners seen here, and the few that are have acquired a country air, a touch of the local.

I pass beyond the houses of Caprile, which descend by degrees and plunge into the fields. Shining amidst these houses, whiter, taller, more striking, preceded by a dense, sombre park, lies the villa where the queen of Sweden used to summer.

The huge windows that give on to the terraces are open. The wind plays with the white curtains hung across the mysteriously shadowed rooms. On the first terrace, an awning unfurled against the sun flaps in the wind that swells it. In the shade of the awning stands a wicker armchair strewn with pillows. Once, seated upon that armchair, the queen awaited her consort's arrival by sea. But now the chair is empty, and the awning whips in the wind, solitary. I hearken back to my distant childhood.

The houses of Caprile gradually sink into the green. At this point, I spy nothing but countryside. The path descends the gentlest slope. The sun blazes more than ever. Trees bloom red and white in the midst of your dark olive grove, Pallas. An old woman, followed by a patient goat, carries a bundle of twigs on her head. She overtakes me and vanishes into the gardens. The path forks: one branch ascends the mountain; the other declines to the sea. Sitting on the edge of a farm, a Nordic adolescent with long hair and bare legs greets me according to the rural custom. To requite his country courtesy, I ask him the direction of the Torre della Guardia. He rises to his feet and nods toward a thicket of trees that closes off the bottom of the path. A few bounds down that narrow stony track bring me to a clearing, near a low wall, which surrounds a small cluster of pine trees and a circular tower commanding the sea.

The sea opens before me on every side. I find two gates, both locked with hefty bolts. Here I feel the need to muster my piratical inclinations. I clamber up the wall and leap down the other side.

The cluster of pines wherein the wind whistles casts an Arcadian shadow around the closed villa, which stares at me suspiciously with its double bow windows. The air smells of resin; the earth is carpeted with yellowed pine needles whereon the foot slips. I try the first door that I encounter, but—good God!—this is a spacious, abandoned *buen retiro* where thousands of lizards slither horribly.

The other doors, which probably give on to places more worthy of visitation, mightily resist my force. The glance that I cast through the misted panes of the low windows reveals nothing but empty rooms and open doors that introduce still more empty rooms. In a corner, between two doorways, a solitary amphora stands upright on its iron tripod. Nonetheless, I do not repress my curiosity to visit the interior. I find a massive entry studded with huge bolts, furnished with a knocker and an enormous key, apparently medieval.

I already imagine myself the master of the mysterious villa. I grasp the end of the enormous key, but it turns uselessly. Alas! The key is pure fiction, an ornament, a prank. And as I swallow the bitter pill of disappointment, I realize that the secrets of the mysterious villa are safeguarded by an English lock that is miniscule, yet much more secure and tenacious than the enormous decorative key.

The Torre della Guardia: it commands the Punta di Carena from a height of two hundred meters. It is sister to the Torre di Damecuta, which in turn commands the Punta di Vitareta and the mouth of the Grotta Azzurra.

Guardia di Capri. The watchtower. The farthest point of the island. From here one need only screw up one's eyes to discover the Pillars of Hercules and the mysterious ocean.

Below, the lighthouse of the Migliera rises over the keeper's red cottage. The sea foams along the jagged coast and, pale offshore, darkens beneath the cliffs.

A vast amphitheater, enclosed within enormous arms of rock, descends by symmetrical steps and near the shore blends with the ruins of ancient cities long since ravaged.

Most sweet and awe-inspiring solitude! But this is yet another ruse. The sky's light is too bright, the sea's sparkle too dazzling, so that at first I am unable to discern the miracle. But as my gaze gradually grows accustomed to the spreading, pulsating glare, I discover, as one discerns the transparency of a window pane, the numberless presence of pirates, buccaneers, and sea rovers who, absorbed and silent, are seated on the steps of the amphitheater.

The black ships—they too are ghosts—have weighed anchor. But their crews, inured in their piratical fierceness, listen to the voice of their master who, brandishing a shining scimitar, speaks a language that at this point no one can understand.

I follow the road that, before reaching the Punta di Tragara, passes nearby the Faraglioni.

My ears echo with the usual question concerning the meaning of the word "Faraglioni."

It was not tailor-made for the two famous rocks that emerge off the southern coast of Capri; it is a mariner's term. The huge rocks that rise just offshore the Sicilian village of Aci Castello are also called Faraglioni.

The road that I follow is one of the most elegant on Capri, flanked by the most burgeoning gardens, the most bedecked terraces, the most flamboyant dwellings. Wherever one looks, the predominant kind of roof is the semicircular vault or flattened dome.

This is one of the most distinctive characteristics of Caprese building. It answers to a precise practical exigency. In view of the water shortage on the island, the inhabitants are forced to rely on special cisterns to collect the rainwater that drains off the roofs.

Yet in the case of the modern houses, all more or less in harmony with traditional Caprese architecture (even though the traditional may be slightly deformed by Sezessionist and Futurist echoes), the vaulted roof has acquired a significance that is purely decorative or "local color." Indeed, I find it difficult to believe that the wealthy aesthetes who flock to build their nests on the island of the Sirens prefer rainwater to the costly wines and the mineral waters that repose in the coolness of their cellars.

Suddenly, the pompous entrance of a villa—but what

am I saying? villa? palazzo!—arrests my attention. A plaque affixed to the wall advises that upon paying a token sum one can enter the "Museo Quo Vadis" to admire the Roman historical paintings produced on a grand scale by the Polish artist Jan Styka.

Might this be an occasion to linger? No. To avoid seeing *The Burning of Rome* and *Nero's Song*, I hightail it.

But painting becomes my torment. When in fact the road has broken free of the Futurist constructions and runs bare along the clamorous cliff, I trip over the legs of a slender easel, before which a robust young man wearing a smock ardently paints beneath the admiring gaze of his female companion who is *coiffée* with a jockey's cap.

I inadvertently glance at the canvas, and in the midst of huge cobalt splotches, sky and sea, I recognize the soft ochre of the Faraglioni. O Providence! The robust young man's painting has rendered me the same service that the rearview mirror renders tram drivers.

And sure enough, down below, not painted but natural, stand those famous Gothic cathedrals, proudly lifting their spires and arches from the sea. The water plays and laps against them, emerald in the shady spots, glittering lamé wherever the sun strikes it.

Just as the Three Musketeers are four, so do the "two" Faraglioni amount to four. But the first two, which an ungrateful fate holds fast on the beach, cannot claim the right to bear the name that has rendered these rocks famous. A Faraglione on dry land is a Faraglione no more. It is a painting without a frame. In the decorum of the Faraglioni, the surrounding sea assumes the greatest importance.

I would love to have a go at the arch that perforates the largest of the Faraglioni. I would love to pass through it in a dinghy, like a thread through a needle's eye. But where is the dinghy? I draw away from those rocks, repressing an unsatisfied desire. Amen!

Now the mysterious dog comes on stage. We met at the corner of the hotel. The Quisisana. He is an ordinary mutt, lacking a master as well as a pedigree, with a scrap of rope tied around his neck. His fleas drive him mad, infect him with a kind of delirium tremens. The fact that he divined my intention to climb the Castiglione is beyond question. He starts to scamper before me, marking out a trail. At a fork he stops and barks furiously so as to make me understand that I have taken the wrong direction. I continue just the same. The dog foams with rage, bites stones, and is on the verge of hurling himself upon me.

He was right. The road narrows, coming to an end at a circular belvedere which commands the island on one side and the limitless sea on the other.

Seen from up here, with the huge church crouching over the cloister enclosed within squalid, deserted porticoes, the Certosa di San Giacomo seems like an architectural project that time and dust have reduced to sheer seediness.

In the midst of the revolving, delusive, and pagan panorama of Capri, this vast monastic edifice displays the dark mien of a displaced creature. No: in place of the Certosa, my imagination prefers to evoke the imperial palace that once rose over the same walls. In 1371, states the chronicle, Giacomo Arcucci, to absolve himself from the vow he had made in his endeavor to produce offspring, erected this monastery with the help of Queen Giovanna.

Farther below, the flower beds of the Giardini Augustus border upon the beginning of a severe, militaristic road which was constructed, appropriately enough, by the German armaments manufacturer Krupp.

But the dog must be satisfied. I retrace my steps and start off again down the correct road, but as I am about to saunter through an ancient-looking granite gate, without expecting anything untoward, three sordid little creatures besiege me like tiny Furies and, in an obscurely threatening manner of speech, demand some kind of toll. "Don't you see?" clamors one of them, pointing a filthy digit. My eye pursues the line sketched by that gesture, and only then, on a poster tacked to the inner frame of the gate, do I read these words: "La plus belle rue de Capri. Entrée: 0.50." I fork over the modest tribute and resume following the mysterious dog who, having already bounded up to the peak of the Castiglione, summons me with his most festive barking.

The foundations of the ancient palace are already visible on the surface of the mountain: the mutilated remains of walls and vaults emerge amongst the wild shrubbery like the hulls of old ships shrouded in seaweed. Then, just beyond, I encounter the vast labyrinth where the ruins of the imperial palace intermingle with those of the medieval castle.

The mysterious dog, driven by an impatient joy that I fail to explain, conducts me through empty courtyards, down forlorn corridors strewn with deep grassy carpets, beneath roof vaults split down the center, before horrible windows that gaze into darkness where I discover my face reflected in the black mirror of a still pool, along arches that open onto the distant gulf commanded by Vesuvius, inside three rooms of recent construction in which sadness and solitude reign absolute, amidst the still-fresh signs of a life extinguished scarcely yesterday.

Outside, the mysterious dog barks naggingly.

I exit at the rear of the castle, in a clearing open on every side; the dog sits there, his paws positioned on the edge.

I approach, look, and immediately withdraw in horror: the rock plummets straight to the sea.

The dog howls, summoning me.

Can I still be skeptical? The mysterious dog, in which the spirit of Tiberius certainly lives again, would be pleased to see me hurl headlong down that terrifying cliff.

It would have been a fate that eluded understanding.

After miraculously escaping from the adventure with the dog Tiberius, I leave you to imagine my anxiety as I set about exploring the sites where the memory of Claudius Tiberius Nero is more vividly immortalized—namely, the castle and tower that overlook the eastern point of Capri.

Neverthless, I started once again from the town of Capri, and, fortified with courage, I clambered up the road that takes its name precisely from Tiberius.

Monte Solaro, the great regulator and dam of light, was already spreading its paternal shadow over the underlying valley. On every side the sea stirred most gently beneath the delicate afternoon sky. My resounding step on the venerable Roman stones drew me near the dark heap of ruins, whose moldering vaults and large fragments of mosaic pavement stretched over the slope.

As I inched up the hill, vast rooms opened before my feet,

as well as subterranean cavities wherein the obscure cult of Mithras was once celebrated. Narrow, lengthy corridors snaked between rooms, huge dilapidated vaults displayed the stratification of stone and brick, and a broad mosaic gradient descended toward the sea from this terrible refuge.

Up here fate does not graze the earth but lies suspended between sky and sea. It is all too obvious why Tiberius chose this summit to vent his monstrous manias. "The island," writes Suetonius, the great scandalmonger of imperial life, "pleased him exceedingly because one could land only through a single narrow harbor, and it was surrounded by sheer rocky cliffs and deep sea."

I gaze out over the horrifying precipice, whence the intractable ruler was wont to hurl any displeasing subject with a kick in the arse.

How much time did I spend bent over the Salto di Tiberio? I couldn't tell. I realized my enchantment only when the reason that had provoked it became clear to me. My propitious star willed that fear would conquer my curiosity. Yet that curiosity—how difficult to free oneself from it! From the depths of the abyss where every sense of distance had vanished, I heard a question rise, gentle yet insistent. In the void that lay beyond the cliff, Death was singing in peerless tones. She spoke in a maternal voice, inspiring more faith than any living thing. Who would stop me from surrendering myself to her?

The malefactor kills to try his hand, to test on others what he would perform on himself. If Tiberius sent slaves hurling down from this cliff, he was only momentarily repressing the terrible, nagging desire to throw himself from the Salto di Tiberio.

What great temptation, what perfect instrument has nature constructed for the malefactor at this utmost point of Capri! And how sagacious of the Capresi to have erected—on the exact same spot—a statue to the Madonna del Soccorso, Our Lady of Deliverance!

Let us give thanks to those pious builders. The Salto di Tiberio is now "disinfected." Today sailors of the Tyrrhenian lift their thankful eyes to the gentle simulacrum of the Mother of God, just as at other times sailors of the Aegean lifted their trusting gaze to the statue of Pallas Athena shining on the rock of the Athenian Acropolis.

Altogether consoled, I enter the church that rises triumphant upon the ruins of extinct pagandom. At the sides of the simple, bare altar, two tiny caravels—the thankful gift of mariners rescued from Neptune's ire—spread yellowed sails in the soft half-light of the Christian temple.

"And I, Mother of Consolation, when shall I offer you my tiny votive caravel?"

Thus I was thinking as I descended the road which, just a brief while before, I had climbed with so many misivings, with so much apprehension.

By now I am no longer fearful of an encounter with Tiberius's ghost. As if to fortify the beneficent effect of the Madonna del Soccorso, when I reach the fork that leads, on the one hand, to the Arco Naturale and, on the other, to the Semaphore of the Tuoro Grande, I find a little chapel before which burns a sacred lamp. The dedication is worded thus: "Matromania alla Madre del Divin Amore."

How strange the fate of words! "Matromania," wherein one can perceive the obscure trace of "madre," is nothing but a deformation of "Mitromania," which in turn is nothing but a development of the name "Mithras." Yet to discover what little remains of the ancient Persian cult of the sun god, should we descend the hundred or so rock-carved steps to penetrate the pitch-black grotto of Mitromania?

No. Night falls. My stride involuntarily leads me to the left. The wind howls frightfully within the rocky gorge. On the hermetic facade of an abandoned cottage, the words "Tea Room" are blazoned in black, redoubling the desolation of the place. The black sea screams enraged at the bottom of the craggy basin. The Arco Naturale lifts its titanic vault against the leaden eastern sky. Here would lie the cadavers of those who vainly attempted to violate the inaccessible peak—if they hadn't been swallowed by the black mouths of the caves gaping amongst the rocks. But why does a tragic fragment of rope dangle whistling in the wind?

Fate had resolved otherwise. When I believed I had distanced myself from every peril, some unknown demon led me back to the western part of the Island of Iron. In the shadow of night falling from sky to sea, I spied the ghost of Claudius Tiberius Nero rising before me. We were near a tumbledown tower.

Neither he nor I spoke. Locked in a desperate struggle, we both plummeted into the mouth of the blackest well, which seemed well-nigh bottomless.

Of that precipitous subterranean journey, the only memory that rekindles in me is the moment at which I felt the cool touch of water on my hands.

My hands were silvery. Above me stretched a vast vault, wherein innumerable blue eyes opened intermittently.

More eyes, likewise blue, were spread about me but so densely packed as to weave some sort of magic carpet, which gently pulsed in the slow undulation of the calmed sea.

Then, in the silence of the grotto, the voice of Clio rose:

"Banish your every wonder. This is the Grotta Azzurra. You have tumbled down here through the subterranean passageway that once joined this grotto to the imperial villa of Damecuta. In that epoch, the motherless emperor descended to these depths, accompanied by a cortège of hetaerae, and the fires of their bestial orgies blazed within these granite walls. But now every peril has passed. Enter this bark and sail off."

Thus spoke the goddess of History, and I complied with her command. I bowed my head as I emerged from the Grotta Azzurra, and shortly thereafter, in the midst of the measureless sea, I eyed the towering ghost of the Island of Iron slowly fading in the night.

Adieu! Adieu!

(1934)

My Civil Death

Massimo Bontempelli

WHY, DEAR GOD, did you make me so sensitive? Without this imperfection, I would be a millionaire today. And in fact I was very rich for some time. But because of my extreme sensitivity, I had to give up my wealth. I was rich after the sudden triumph of my performance in the film *A Civil Death*. By chance I had reached the Olympus of silent-film actors, and of necessity I had to leave it.

I lived in a village in Calabria. One day I was talking to a waiter in a café there, and no sooner had he left than a gentleman sitting at the next table introduced himself to me. He had an American accent.

"I'm a director with the Celestial Dumbplay Studio. I just heard you talking to the waiter, and I noticed you have the makings of a fine silent-film actor."

He went on to say that my appearance seemed particu-

Born in Como, MASSIMO BONTEMPELLI *(1878–1960) wrote novels, stories, plays, and essays, all of which reveal his inclination toward modernist experiments. In a polemic entitled* The Twentieth-Century Adventure *(1938), he advocated magic realism. A recent translation of his work is* Separations: Two Novels of Mothers and Children *(2000).*

larly appropriate for the male lead in the film version of *A Civil Death,* the famous play by the nineteenth-century dramatist Paolo Giacometti. In fact, it was to shoot the film that he had come to Calabria, the setting of the play.

I hesitated. He insisted and offered me a prodigious sum. A few days later we began working. At once I immersed myself in the volcanic personality of the Sicilian protagonist, Corrado, a painter and impassioned lover who murdered his brother-in-law in a fit of anger. But I entered too deeply. I lost myself in him. For Corrado, the action is a series of intense and often agonizing experiences: love, jealousy, hatred, murder, imprisonment, escape, marital strife, and parental anguish, all of which force him to embrace a civil death—suicide. While I was acting, I felt every one of these tempests as if they were real. After each exhausting effort—that is, after each scene—I had to undergo a still greater effort, followed by long periods of rest, in order to clear my mind of its disturbed state and prepare for another day's shooting. This process wasted much time, but my interpretation of the role was such a huge success that the director gladly put up with the delays.

The work proceeded calmly as long as I was playing Corrado before his easel amid the wild, natural scenery or in his meetings with Rosalia at the beginning of their affair. But her family didn't want me.

For a little while I remained truly angry with the kind actor who played Rosalia's brother. Nonetheless, after the scene ended, I quickly managed to calm myself down. Then we began filming my abduction of the young girl, and I carried her away before the cyclopean eye of the camera. The zeal that had possessed me was so great that I kept on running and running, quite far from the set, until I leaped over a hedge as the leading lady screamed in my arms. In the end my coworkers had to restrain me. Who knows where I would have carried her if they hadn't over-taken me and snapped me out of it, plunging me back into innocent reality.

The most painful part of my torture began with the scene in which I murdered my brother-in-law. That day I hated him with a passion. I killed him by smashing his skull with a huge club. (Fortunately, the editor left only the beginning of my action, my hand rising with the weapon.) I had become a wild animal, so they took me to a sanitar-ium and had me treated. For several weeks I trembled with hatred. I wasn't crazy. I knew perfectly well that my good friend wasn't the brother of Mara d'Ayala (my leading lady's stage name), and he wouldn't have cared in the least if I had married her twice a day. Within me, in my nerves, in my blood, I felt every shudder of hatred that Corrado felt for his brother-in-law, but in my mind I was very much aware that I wasn't Corrado. This superimposition of Cor-rado's personality over mine, along with the experience of hatred without object—indeed, of hateless hatred—was even more lacerating.

After I returned to work I acted in the next scene, in which policemen seize me, tie me up, drag me away, and then throw me into prison.

Corrado's thirteen-year prison sentence (a morning's work) really wore me down, but a few weeks of wholesome nourishment restored my strength so I could carry out my celebrated escape from prison. When I had descended the rugged sides of a tower with the classic knotted sheets and my foot touched the ground, I was free and alone on the open plain. As I joyfully opened my arms before the camera, I felt all the impetuous wind of creation blow into my face from the lens. Then, with my lungs full of air and my eyes turned heavenward, I began to march across the boundless plain.

"Cut!" shouted the director after I had taken a few steps. "Now you've got to act like you're exhausted."

I obeyed. And very rapidly fatigue conquered all my limbs, invading and crushing me.

"That's great. You can get up now. How about acting like a victim of starvation for me?"

I began to gesture and swoon as if I were starving. At once an excruciating hunger tormented my stomach. I felt completely empty, and like a punctured balloon I collapsed and fell to the ground. The workers on the set ran to help me up, but at this point I couldn't stand any longer. I stammered faintly, "F-f-f-food . . ."

They ran to the kitchen tents, brought me plates heaped with rare roast beef and thick slices of bread and cheese and pitchers filled with wine, and I devoured everything— Corrado hadn't eaten in two days. I ate voraciously, in great haste and without interruption for I don't know how long, and finally I regained life and strength.

"Now let's start shooting that scene again—quick, before we lose the light."

I stood up amid the empty plates, refreshed and full, and, gulping down the last mouthful, I ran to the camera.

The director said, "Let's get a close-up of that hungry look on your face. It seemed so real. Do you want to try it again?"

I was brought before the camera. At one meter from the lens, between two white screens which the workers held under my face to focus the light there, I resumed the grimaces. They lasted only a minute, but immediately I felt their effects.

"Very good," said the American. "That's all for now."

But I had again slumped to the ground with weakness. Once more as a result of that famished expression on my face, I was actually suffering from starvation. My stomach gurgled unhappily, empty, stabbed by hunger pains. I begged. Perplexed, the workers had to bring me more to eat, and for a good while I again consumed food and drink like a deluge, a fire.

I needn't go through the entire film up to Corrado's spasmodic death by strychnine. A more detailed account would postpone the amazing events that happened to me later, when the film had been finished for some time and was starting to be sent to theaters around the world.

They *were* amazing events. Incredible, even. Certainly, if someone had told me about them, I would have found him hard to believe. But I have no choice except to believe events that I myself experienced.

When the tormenting work was finished, I felt empty rather than exhausted, as if my soul had become a void. The actors had all left, and the American too had departed with his equipment and I don't how many kilometers of film, but not without leaving me an enormous sum of money and promising me more when prints were sold. He was very enthusiastic about the prospects for *A Civil Death*.

Time passed, and I didn't think about the American and his film anymore. However, that sense of emptiness, of internal nothingness persisted in me. I no longer had any desires or feelings and hardly any sensations at all. (But every so often, at irregular intervals, I experienced brief attacks of confusion and anxiety that I could not explain. Still, they subsided immediately.)

One day, at the beginning of September, I received a very amiable letter from the American, telling me that he was in Rome. He added, "The film has finally been edited, and it has turned out to be quite beautiful. We shall give it a trial screening on the fifteenth of this month. I hope you will come to see it then." This letter left me cold. After a few days I answered that it was impossible for me to go to Rome on the fifteenth. On the fourteenth, I boarded the train and went to Rome.

The American gave me a warm welcome, but, notwithstanding how much I wanted to return his cordiality, I couldn't overcome my indifference. I asked him very firmly not to introduce me to anyone. I arrived at the theater with him and hid myself in the back, alone, in a dark corner. Only about twenty people had been invited, and they were sitting in the middle of the theater. The lights went out, and on the screen began the story of Corrado.

I had not foreseen what would happen.

I wasn't interested at the beginning, but as soon as the first scenes were over and Corrado appeared on the screen, I felt I had leaped out of the pallid languor in which I had been immersed ever since work on the film had ended. It was as if I had fallen unconscious and was suddenly revived, or as if I were some inanimate substance that had instantly jumped from nothingness into being at the touch of a god. All this happened in a moment, the moment when I saw the image of Corrado—that is, my image—calmly seated before an easel in the middle of a field. But a second later, in a flash of insight, I realized that the resurrection I had just experienced didn't occur in me, that it was in him, in that man who was now gazing at Rosalia with radiant devotion; yet although this emotion was expressed in his face, I felt it in me entirely. Much to my surprise, I suddenly found myself holding out my arms in the darkness of the theater, transported by our passionate love.

Then my image disappeared, and I felt empty again. In the same breath a violent rage possessed me, while on the screen Corrado—or rather I—argued bitterly with Rosalia's obstinate family. From this point on, there was a crescendo of anguish interrupted by brief intervals of emptiness. Everything that Corrado had suffered in the course of twenty years—and that I had acted out in a few months—was now condensed into two horrible hours.

When Corrado finally rolled on the floor, fitfully jerking under the influence of the strychnine, I found myself lying on my back between the seats, writhing in pain, nearly dying. Suddenly the lights went on, and I was empty and motionless. The audience crowded around the director. Before they discovered me, I left the shadow of my corner, exited through a side door, and headed for my hotel. That same evening, the American found me and told me about everyone's enthusiasm.

"We have already sold a print for Rome, one for Milan, and one in France. The film will premiere in Rome on Thursday, at the Splendor Theater, and next month it will open in Milan."

He handed me a check. The following day he returned with two new contracts, which he pushed me to sign, and left me still more money.

I left Rome for my village, but without any hope of recovery. I had become empty once again. And now I was very much aware of my terrible predicament. I wasn't too confident that I could escape it simply by refraining from watching my performance in *A Civil Death*. I understood perfectly that my life and sensibility had passed entirely into those two kilometers of film, and there they remained, still tied by some mysterious thread to their source in my heart. I understood beyond any possible doubt that every time the film was shown, anywhere in the world, I would feel its different phases and effects repeated in me during the screening.

In fact, a few days later, while I was sitting in my room at four in the afternoon, I wasn't amazed to feel the vigorous air of the countryside blowing around my head (it was the countryside where I was painting, far away in Rome on the screen of the Splendor Theater), and then I underwent my amorous transports for Rosalia, followed by the arguments, my insane anger, my imprisonment and escape. How I wept for joy, sitting alone at the table, once again holding my wife in my arms! Next I felt the entire horrible sequel of tortures, jealousy, the loss of human dignity—how I sobbed in my empty room when my daughter was frightened and drew back in horror from me! And a few minutes later I rolled convulsively on the floor. This attack lasted two hours, and almost immediately it began again. I had to endure Corrado's fate four times between four in the afternoon and midnight, at regular intervals, conforming with the screenings in the Splendor Theater five hundred kilometers away. And the next day, and every day thereafter, from four in the afternoon until midnight, four times a day, the performances continued.

I took a train and returned to Rome. (I was careful to travel at night and in the morning so I wouldn't be seized by those ridiculous attacks on the train when the film was being screened.) The distinguished doctor to whom I had turned for help wanted to observe my daily attacks repeatedly, until he was able to recognize the perfect synchronism of my movements, internal and external, during the period of each screening. On the sixth of October things grew more complicated.

At four o'clock that day, I seemed to notice a greater intensity in my sensations from the outset. After a few minutes they felt confused in strange ways; at a certain point, they were all mixed up and absurdly connected. The distinguished doctor said, "This is the beginning of a beneficial crisis." I, on the other hand, immediately understood what was happening and shouted, "Today, today it's being screened in Milan too!"

The film began again, and the confused sensations also began again. The two screenings were superimposed within me. In Milan, the intervals between each screening were shorter, and their speed was slightly faster. While (in Rome) my arms were delivering the murderous blow to my brother-in-law, my knees (in Milan) were nervously knocking together at the prospect of freedom as I climbed down the side of the prison tower. A little later my body violently jerked on the floor, while my face smiled with joy as I contemplated my newborn daughter. After midnight the attacks ceased, and the distinguished doctor asked me to take a walk with him. At Piazza Colonna we ran into the American, who was ecstatic to see me.

"We've sold ten more prints—in America and Sweden. The film's going to be a big hit everywhere. Within a couple of weeks it will be shown simultaneously, in Italy and abroad, at twenty theaters—twenty—just think of it!"

I screamed with horror.

I resorted to the only possible remedy: I bought every print of *A Civil Death*, as well as the negative. The American was sick over it. I burned them all and returned to my village.

Since I didn't make enough money from the American, I raised the necessary sum by selling my sensitive heart to a medical school—for use after my death, of course. The distinguished doctor insists that the autopsy will be most interesting, and actually it was he who made the school pay me a considerable amount. I'm not at all ashamed to mention this transaction; in fact, I want everyone to know that my sensitive heart has already been sold and is no longer available.

(1925)

The Black Kid
Luigi Pirandello

UNDOUBTEDLY, Signor Charles Trockley is right. I am in fact prepared to admit that Signor Charles Trockley can never be wrong, because he and reason are one and the same thing. His every movement, every glance, every word are so rigid and precise, so considered and certain, that no one can fail to recognize it is impossible for Signor Charles Trockley—on whatever topic you choose, no matter what question is posed to him or incident befalls him—to be in the wrong.

He and I, to cite an example, were born in the same year, the same month, and nearly on the same day, he in England, I in Sicily. Today, the fifteenth of June, he completes his forty-eighth year; I shall complete mine on the twenty-eighth. Fine. Yet ask him how old we shall be next year, he

LUIGI PIRANDELLO *(1867–1936) was born in Agrigento. An innovative playwright, novelist, and short-story writer, he won the Nobel Prize for Literature in 1934. Pirandello was a master of irony who experimented with dramatic and narrative forms, often using stories as the basis for plays. His novels,* The Late Mattia Pascal *(1904) and* One, No One and One Hundred Thousand *(1926), have appeared in English.*

on the fifteenth and I on the twenty-eighth of June. Signor
Trockley is not at a loss; he doesn't hesitate for a minute;
with unwavering confidence he asserts that next year, on
the fifteenth and twenty-eighth of June, he and I will be
one year older, which is to say forty-nine.

Is it possible to prove Signor Charles Trockley wrong?

Time doesn't pass the same way for everyone. In a single day, a single hour, I could suffer greater harm than he
has for the past ten years, given the rigorous discipline that
maintains his well-being; because of the lamentable disor-
der of my spirit, I could live—during this year—more
than an entire life. My body, weaker and less scrupulously
cared for than Signor Trockley's, has deteriorated during
these forty-eight years as much as his body will no doubt
deteriorate in seventy. Indeed, even though his hair has
turned a fine shade of silver, his face retains the flush of
youth, utterly devoid of wrinkles, and he can still fence
every morning with youthful agility.

Well, what does it matter? To Signor Charles Trockley,
all of these considerations, whether hypothetical or factual,
are pointless and far removed from reason. Reason tells
Signor Charles Trockley that, when all is said and done,
next year, on the fifteenth and twenty-eighth of June, he
and I will be one year older, which is to say forty-nine.

This being the case, listen to what recently happened to
Signor Trockley and try, if you can, to prove him wrong.

A year ago this past April, following the usual itinerary
sketched by Baedeker for an Italian trip, Miss Ethel Holloway, the very young and very vivacious daughter of Sir
W. H. Holloway, a very rich and very influential English

peer, arrived in Sicily, at Agrigento, to visit the marvelous remains of the ancient Doric city. Attracted by the enchanting strand, which during that month is rife with white almond blossoms in the warm breath of the African sea, she decided to spend more than one night in the grand Hôtel des Temples, which stands outside of today's poor, precipitous city, in the open countryside, a most pleasant site.

For twenty-two years, Signor Charles Trockley has been the English vice-consul at Agrigento. And for twenty-two years, every day, at sunset, he has strolled with his elastic, measured step from the town high on the hill to the ruins of the Akragantine temples, ethereal and majestic on the uneven ridge that interrupts the nearby slope of the acropolis. Here once rose the splendid marble of the ancient city that Pindar extolled as the most beautiful among mortal cities.

The ancients used to say that the Akragantines ate every day as if they were to die tomorrow but constructed their houses as if they would never die. They eat little now, because of the crushing poverty in the town and countryside, and after so many wars, seven fires, and an equal number of sackings, there remains no trace of the houses that formed the ancient city. In their place stands a wood of almond and Saracen olive trees, which is therefore called the Bosco della Civita, the Civic Forest. And the leafy, ash-colored olive trees march in procession to the columns of the majestic temples, where they seem to pray for peace to descend on those abandoned slopes. Beneath the ridge runs, when it can, the river Akragas, which Pindar glorified as rich in flocks. Some herds of goats still cross the stony river bed; they clamber up the rocky ridge to stretch out and graze on the meager pasture in the solemn shadow of the still-intact Tempio della Concordia. The brutish goatherd also lies down on the steep steps of the pronaos (or atrium), drowsy as an Arab, and draws a plaintive air from his reed flute.

To Signor Charles Trockley, the intrusion of the goats into the temple has always seemed a horrible profanation; and on countless occasions he has made formal complaints to the custodians of the monuments, although without obtaining any response but a smile of philosophical indulgence and a shrug. Truly trembling with indignation, Signor Charles Trockley has griped about these smiles and shrugs when I sometimes accompany him on his daily stroll. It often happens that in the Tempio della Concordia or, farther on, in the incomplete Tempio di Giunone or in the temple popularly called the Tempio dei Giganti, Signor Trockley meets with a band of his compatriots who have come to visit the ruins. And he never fails to call their attention—with that indignation which neither time nor habit has placated or diminished in the slightest—to the profanation represented by the goats lying and grazing in the shade of the columns. To tell the truth, however, not all the English visitors share Signor Trockley's indignation. Many have in fact perceived a certain poetry in the goats' repose at the temples, which now remain solitary in the midst of the great, oblivious countryside. More than one visitor, much to the horror of Signor Trockley, has displayed not a little joy and admiration at that sight.

That April, no one displayed more joy and admiration than the very young and very vivacious Miss Ethel Holloway. In fact, just as the indignant vice-consul began to inform her of several remarkable archaeological details, to which neither Baedeker nor the other guidebooks had yet assigned the proper value, Miss Ethel Holloway committed the indiscretion of suddenly turning her back to him so as to run after a charming black kid that had been born a few days before. The kid gamboled here and there among the reclining goats as if so many fireflies danced in the air about him, and he seemed to be astonished by his own bold yet unbalanced leaps, since the faintest sound, the slightest breeze, the tiniest shadow, in what was still to him the uncertain spectacle of life, set him trembling and shaking all over with timidity.

On that day I was with Signor Trockley, and even though I was most pleased with the delight felt by the little miss, who was so quickly enamored of the black kid as to want to buy it at any cost, I was also most sorry that she caused so much suffering to poor Signor Charles Trockley.

"Do you really wish to buy the kid?"

"Yes, yes, I want to buy it at once! At once!"

And the little miss trembled all over too, just like that adorable black animal, likely without imagining—not even faintly—that she might have greatly annoyed Signor Trockley, who had fiercely hated those beasts for so long.

In vain did Signor Trockley endeavor to dissuade her, to force her to consider all the trouble that would result from that purchase. He had to yield in the end, and, out of respect for her father, he approached the boorish goatherd to arrange for the acquisition of the black kid.

Miss Ethel Holloway, after paying for the purchase, told

Signor Trockley that she would entrust her kid to the director of the Hôtel des Temples, and that later, upon her arrival in London, she would telegraph to have the adorable animal delivered to her as soon as possible, all expenses paid. She then returned to the hotel by carriage, with the kid bleating and wriggling in her arms.

I saw—against the sun setting amid an amazing embellishment of fantastic clouds, all ablaze over a sea that shone beneath them like a boundless golden mirror—I saw the black carriage drawing away with that young blond woman, delicate yet passionate, infused with a nimbus of radiant light; and it seemed almost a dream to me. Then I realized that since she could immediately conceive such an intense desire, no, such an intense affection for that little black kid, even though far away from her native country and her habitual attitudes and feelings, she mustn't possess even a scrap of the sturdy reason that governs with so much gravity the actions and thoughts, steps and words of Signor Charles Trockley.

And so what did the little Miss Ethel Holloway have in place of reason?

Nothing more than stupidity, declared Signor Trockley with a barely contained rage, which is well-nigh pitiful in a man like him, always so self-controlled.

The reason for his rage lies in the events that followed upon the purchase of that black kid.

The next day Miss Ethel Holloway departed from Agrigento. From Sicily she traveled to Greece, from Greece to Egypt, from Egypt to the Indies.

Miraculously, upon arriving safe and sound in London at the end of November, after nearly eight months and the many adventures that would inevitably occur during such a long journey, she still remembered the black kid she had bought one distant day amongst the ruins of the Akragantine temples in Sicily.

No sooner did she arrive than, in accordance with the arrangement, she wrote to Signor Charles Trockley to retrieve it.

The Hôtel des Temples closes every year in the middle of June and reopens at the beginning of November. The director, to whom Miss Ethel Holloway had entrusted the kid at her departure in June, had in turn entrusted him to the hotel custodian, although without any instructions, displaying instead more than a little irritation at the inconvenience that the animal had—and still—caused him. From what the director had said, the custodian daily expected the vice-consul to arrive to pick up the kid and dispatch it to England. Yet since he saw no one show up, he thought the best course would be to rid himself of the animal, and so he consigned it to the same goatherd who had made the sale to Miss Holloway, promising that either he would receive it as a gift if, as things appeared, she no longer wished to retrieve it or he would be compensated for his care and pasture in the event that the vice-consul came to inquire after it.

When, after nearly eight months, Miss Ethel Holloway's letter arrived from London, the director of the Hôtel des Temples, the custodian, and the goatherd were all thrown into a sea of confusion—the director for having entrusted the kid to the custodian, the custodian for having entrusted it to the goatherd, and the goatherd for having in turn consigned it to another goatherd with the same promises that the custodian had made him. Concerning the whereabouts of this second goatherd there was no information. The search lasted more than a month. At last, one fine day, in the office of the vice-consulate at Agrigento, Signor Charles Trockley was presented with a horrible foul-smelling horned beast, whose faded reddish hair was torn and encrusted with mud and excrement and who, with his head lowered threateningly, emitted a deep, hoarse, tremulous bleating as if he were asking what might be wanted of him, reduced to that state by the necessity of things, in a place so alien to his habits.

Well, Signor Trockley, as usual, was not in the least daunted by such a sight; he didn't waver for a moment. He took account of the time that had elapsed, from the beginning of April to the end of December, and he concluded, most reasonably, that the charming black kid of the past could very well be this filthy beast of the present. And without the slightest hesitation he replied to Miss Holloway that he would dispatch it at once from Porto Empedocle on the first English merchant steamer returning to England. From the neck of that horrible animal he hung a tag with her address and ordered that it be transported to the coast. He himself, seriously jeopardizing his dignity, used a rope to drag the fractious beast to the pier, followed by a gang of urchins. He then loaded it on board the departing steamship and returned to Agrigento, most confident of having scrupulously fulfilled the obligation that he had assumed, not because of Miss Ethel Holloway's deplorable frivolity, but because of the respect due to her father.

Yesterday Signor Charles Trockley came to my home in such a mental and physical state that, extremely dismayed, I at once rushed to support him, lead him to a chair, bring him a glass of water.

"For the love of God, Signor Trockley, what happened to you?"

Still incapable of speaking, he drew a letter from his pocket and handed it to me.

It was from Sir W. H. Holloway, the English peer, and it contained a string of forceful insults for the affront that Signor Trockley had dared to offer his daughter Miss Ethel by sending her that filthy, frightful beast.

Herewith the thanks that poor Signor Trockley received for the trouble he had taken.

But what did the stupid Miss Ethel Holloway expect? Did she expect that some eleven months after her purchase the same black kid would arrive in London, the same frisky animal, small and bright, trembling all over with timidity amid the columns of the ancient Greek temple in Sicily? Could this be possible? Signor Charles Trockley couldn't resign himself to it.

Seeing him before me in that state, I started to comfort him as best I could, agreeing that truly Miss Ethel Holloway must be a creature who was not only capricious, but unspeakably irrational.

"Stupid! Stupid! Stupid!"

"Let's rather say irrational, Signor Trockley, my dear friend. But you see"—I permitted myself to add timidly—

"she left that April with the charming image of the black kid in her eyes and mind, and she couldn't—let's be fair—put a good face (as irrational as she is) on the reason that you, Signor Trockley, unexpectedly set before her by sending that monstrous goat."

"What then?" he asked, rising to his feet and casting a hostile glance at me. "What should I have done, in your view?"

"I wouldn't like, Signor Trockley," I hastened to answer him, embarrassed, "I wouldn't like to seem irrational as well, like that little miss from your distant country, but if I had been in your shoes, do you know what I would have done? Either I would have replied to Miss Ethel Holloway that the charming black kid had died from want of her kisses and caresses, or I would have bought another one, tiny and bright, similar in every way to the kid she bought last April, and I would have sent it to her, very confident that Miss Ethel Holloway would never imagine that her kid couldn't be preserved in exactly the same condition for eleven months. In suggesting this course, you see, I do acknowledge that Miss Ethel Holloway is the most irrational creature in the world, and that, as always, reason resides wholly on your side, Signor Trockley, my dear friend."

(1913)

The Shawl

Maria Messina

MARIANGELINA couldn't be called beautiful, but she was young, and she had the blackest hair and sky-blue eyes that were like two flowers, two periwinkles just opening. Her tiny plump figure possessed a lively, energetic air that called to mind sparrows when they perch on eaves and turn their little heads to and fro, never stopping for a moment.

Anyone who passed through the Vicolo della Méndola, at any hour whatsoever, might hear the voice of Mariangelina the dressmaker twittering and humming. She was a happy soul. The days used to flit by because she would sing and because, if she fell silent, the thoughts that passed through her head weren't unpleasant and didn't stop, just like a swarm of bright butterflies over the first spring blossoms.

Born in Palermo in 1887, MARIA MESSINA *spent time in Umbria, Tuscany, the Marches, and Naples, but always wrote about Sicily. Although early in her career her work met with critical acclaim, she died forgotten in 1944. Several decades later she was rediscovered by the Sicilian writer Leonardo Sciascia, who viewed her as an Italian Katherine Mansfield. Her novel* A House in the Shadows *(1921) is available in English. This story is characteristic of Messina's concern with the constricted lives of her female protagonists.*

And indeed another woman, in her shoes, might have done nothing but weep day and night! Her father had died. Her feeble-minded sister lived at home, the poor thing. She wasn't bothersome, but it was heartrending to see her play with remnants of fabric in some nook, worse than a three-year-old. And her mother . . . it was enough to mention her mother's name, Nera. Everyone in the village was acquainted with her and knew how little she was worth because she trailed a chain that bound her to Don Giuanni, even when her unfortunate husband was alive.

But Mariangelina wasn't familiar with this sad story, because in truth Nera had always nurtured a great respect for her daughter, and she had never permitted Don Giuanni to set foot in her home. Since Mariangelina was known to be an honest young woman, not only the burgisi but also many ladies would summon her when they needed a frock to be cut. But they wanted her alone. Nera, who did not need to be told, used to accompany her daughter to the gate and then return to collect her without ever approaching the house.

"Rich people's houses embarrass me," she explained when her daughter asked her why she wouldn't let herself be seen.

She couldn't ever forget that after sullying her name she might lose her livelihood, poor creature! At least in this way she would have work, if nothing else. She had acquired a fine clientele. Not like the Ragusa sisters—she couldn't expect that!—but a decent business that included dealings with Donna Mimi Singani, for example, and the baroness's niece. When Mariangelina would go to cut, she couldn't sing, of course. But she talked. And she talked a blue streak. Her client, who stood before her like a watchful carabiniere—so that she didn't make a botch of the cloth!—would have to remind her every so often:

"Mariangeli' . . . Do you intend to keep me here till nightfall?"

For a moment she would hear only the squeak of the huge scissors. Then she lifted her head and said very seriously:

"Signora, what would you think if I wore a shawl?"

Almost two years had passed since she began asking this very question. She used to reckon up the responses. On one side she would put all the noes, those ladies who replied that it wouldn't be proper for a young girl to indulge in such an extravagance; on the other side were all the yeses, those who said that since she was a dressmaker, she could wear a shawl without embarrassment.

"Isn't it true?!" Mariangelina was pleased. "Every woman wears a shawl these days . . . I tell you even Signora Bifara is keen to wear one!"

Then she would look into her client's eyes to see whether the lady was saying yes just to tease her.

Mariangelina couldn't think of anything but the shawl. Whenever she spoke of it, her face reddened with excitement. Yet she wanted it more to honor her craft than to serve any foolish ambition.

As she returned to work, beneath a window that carried the scent of mint and verbena, she put the thought of the shawl behind her. If she had something to sew, she had everything. Gold braid, moiré silk, velvet, razor-thin cloth were her passion. She gazed at the beautiful material with wide eyes; she caressed it for the sheer pleasure of feeling it under her fingers. When she went to cut, she looked straight at the table she had prepared. If her eyes fell upon some cloth that pleased her, she would waste an hour singing its praises:

"How beautiful it is! How fine! I'll make you a dress, Donna Mimi—anyone who sees it will take leave of their senses."

"Chatterbox!" was the response she received. "Start cutting!"

Fabric of poor quality practically aroused her pity; but if the colors suited her taste, she would work cheerfully just the same. When she was fitting a basted dress, she was happy if she could please herself as well as her client. Occasionally, she would propose some alterations. If they didn't listen to her, she wouldn't insist, because she was prudent; but if they followed her advice, she would blush to the ears and then find a way to interject the remark that even in a city she would distinguish herself, with the imagination she had!

She loved her trade. While she was working, she nearly forgot about the shawl. But she needed only to help a lady with her manteau and she would think of it again. At once she would say:

"It's no use . . . One of these days, Signora, you'll see me with a shawl. And then what will you say, Signora?"

She didn't like playing second fiddle to the Ragusa sisters, who weren't as clever as she was and yet served the best ladies of the village. She was terribly fearful that in time even her clients, those of note, would fancy the work of the two sisters who made such a splash, as old and ugly as they were, only because they wore shawls. And so one beautiful morning she entrusted a bit of her little nest egg to Donna Lisa's nephew, who was traveling to Palermo, so that he might buy her a shawl.

"What luxury!" said the young man. "Does the shawl mean, then, that you'll take a beau?"

"Yes," Mariangelina replied merrily. "And you'll be my first Prince Charming . . . Are you pleased?"

Donna Lisa's nephew said this because Mariangelina used to laugh and make mock of all the lads. And indeed if she had wished, they would have walked through that vicolo as if they were strolling down the main street of Sant'Antonio! With Angelo, Donna Lisa's nephew, she would play telegraph, he from the stone balcony beneath the pergola, she from her little window. They could hardly stifle their giggling. Another woman would have passed for a coquette. But everyone was familiar with Mariangelina; they knew that she was a happy soul, a big girl who still possessed the innocence of a child. It was enough to look into her eyes, those eyes that shone with laughter, the color of the sky when it's serene. No one would have called her Nera's daughter!

With the shawl, Mariangelina almost seemed beautiful. Angelo told her that she would have turned heads in Palermo, with that face that begged to be kissed. For the first time, Mariangelina didn't know how to jest at the compliment. Slightly pale, she gazed enraptured at the new shawl unfurled on her arms.

It seemed like an eternity before she could display herself before her clients. She peacocked for a short while, until she grew accustomed to it.

Yet little by little, one at a time, her clients started to leave her.

Mariangelina's idle fancies had gone to her head. Regardless of what she wished, she would always be Nera's daughter; it couldn't be forgotten! As for marriage, that paltry cloth she wore would have stopped any man from marrying her. And with all the foolish ambition she nurtured, she wasn't a girl who would stay in her place. No, no, on the contrary. She would die a beggar!

Donna Mimi, the secretary's wife, and four or five burgisi had remained loyal. Mariangelina was mortified and surprised.

Angelo told her:

"The Ragusa sisters go to Palermo every so often. That just goes to show you! If you want a clientele, you need to get a little dust in your eyes."

On another occasion he told her:

"Did you know a dressmaker *has* to go to Palermo?"

Eventually the idea of going to Palermo entered Mariangelina's head too. First she spoke to her mother about it. Then she began to tell the few ladies who had remained loyal to her, watching their eyes to see what they thought, just as when she felt she had to wear a shawl. It was winter. So as not to go too late, they fixed their departure for the first day of February. And for two months there was talk of nothing else in Mariangelina's house.

When the baggage was packed, Angelo thought that the first cab driver in Palermo might swindle two women so alone. To avoid attracting attention, he departed a day in advance.

What a stir Mariangelina caused! What a celebration! She went to say goodbye to all her clients, even those who had left her some time ago. She offered to run errands for neighbors, promised souvenirs to this one and that. There was talk of nothing else in the Vicolo della Méndola, as if Nera and her daughter were departing for America.

They stayed a week in Palermo. Angelo drove them around like a relative, accompanying them here and there to show them the most beautiful things.

To friends he said that Mariangelina was his sweetheart; but he didn't have the nerve to joke with her as he did back in their village, because he was crushed to see her so awed, so reticent, looking at him with those great big eyes filled with trust. Nera toddled along behind the two young people, her feet killing her. She couldn't keep going; every morning it seemed like an eternity before evening would arrive and she could rest in bed.

Mariangelina, however, never wanted to stop. She seemed to be drunk on the air of Palermo. She didn't think about her village, didn't think that she had come only to see the fashions and would have to return. She even forgot she had promised her neighbors so many trinkets. Clinging to Angelo's arm as he took her here and there, she felt like she was living in the world of fables. No more did she have to deal with her feeble sister, no more did she have work to be delivered, no more did she have to gobble down a morsel while standing or perched on a corner of a table cluttered with fabric and remnants. . . . She walked and walked with no other aim but to see new things; she ate meals served by a waiter wearing a jacket; dazed, exhausted, happy, she returned in the evening to a room that someone had thought to tidy up. How lovely it was to live in the city! The palazzos, the carriages, the shop windows filled with the most beautiful radiant things, the women who passed by so swiftly on thin high heels, leaving behind a trail of perfume—everything grew confused in her mind, and her sleep was animated with the things she had seen during the day, so that when she awoke and went out, she seemed to be still dreaming.

She was nearly silent. She would do everything that Angelo told her to do. She found herself on the train that would take her back to her little village curled up at the foot of the Castello, without knowing how she got there, while amid the bustle of the station Angelo was still giving advice to Nera as he held open the train door.

Her ears were filled with noise, her eyes with colors—a dazzling stream of sparks. The vicolo was dark and narrow; the neighbors made her melancholy, wearing such drab colors. As Nera turned the key in the lock, greeting someone, Mariangelina felt like bursting into tears.

The journey brought her misfortune. The neighbors viewed her with suspicion, perhaps with envy. She found scarcely any work. It was then that the Ragusa sisters—the two vipers—somehow conveyed to Mariangelina that she had grossly erred in wanting to imitate them, that when one bears a dishonored name, one should keep to the straight and narrow if she doesn't want to make people talk!

Mariangelina couldn't believe it. She was unable to utter a single word in response to anyone who accepted these rumors. It was as if an abyss had opened before her eyes. She remained frightened, devastated. She had black days; she wept for no reason; at certain moments she stared at her mother with great big gloomy eyes. Nera likewise gave her daughter downcast looks. They had to say something to each other. They knew it, especially on those eternal, oppressive evenings when her feeble sister dozed on a bench and everything was veiled in silence and they were alone, face to face, working without making a sound, tormented by the same thought. They said nothing to each other. They didn't have the courage or even the time. Yes, the time, because a month had not yet passed—the almond tree behind the old wall at Casa Ruda was in full bloom—before Nera lay down never to rise again. In a few days, before she knew what was happening, she left for the other world, and her breast bore her sad truth beneath her crossed hands.

Marangelina was alone, since her feeble sister couldn't be called company. In the evening, she would leave the lamp to burn throughout the night. If she awoke, she would be fearful of her sister, who slept with her mouth open, laughing even in her sleep, fearful too of the shadows that lengthened and diminished. Yet she wanted that faint red light during the never-ending nights.

The two sisters were dying of hunger. While the feeble one played in a corner, as always, Mariangelina passed hours upon hours with her chin propped up on her hands. No one came knocking on their door. They were alone, abandoned. And there was nothing more melancholy than hearing the vicolo full of the usual noises, the usual voices. . . .

From the half-closed door came waves of warm air; sometimes you could hear a distant shrill cry—the swallows were already returning—or a chirping that was at once deafening and cheerful—the sparrows were building their nests in the old garden and in the eaves of the Rudas' ancient palazzo. Mariangelina felt as if she had been overcome by a powerful languor, her legs trembled, she was always on the point of bursting into tears; perhaps it was the weakness, perhaps the spring. She would think of the great city, seen as in a dream, where women wear beautiful low-cut dresses with lovely little shoes, and they are all rich and all their eyes burn with the light of happiness.

She looked for work. Because for her work was life. But times had taken a turn for the worse. Even Donna Mimì had her maid tell Mariangelina that she didn't need any new dresses that year.

What rotten luck: she had squandered everything to give herself over to idle pleasures with Donna Lisa's nephew! Who knows what remarkable feats she might have performed in Palermo! Not for nothing had the Lord punished her!

In the sweltering evenings, Mariangelina would open her window again. The first thing she saw was Don Angelo, stationed in his old position. They resumed their banter, he from the stone balcony beneath the pergola, she half hidden by the fragrant verbena, but they spoke softly so that the evil-tongued neighbors might not hear. Mariangelina felt a great tenderness. Angelo was gratefully aware of it, as he came back to speak to her, without mockery, recalling the golden years that had passed forever.

The days no longer seemed so desolate to her. She would wait for dusk before she opened the window to see Don Angelo in the dimness, waiting for her beneath the pergola, speaking so softly that only she could hear:

"Buona sera, Mariangeli'!"

One evening, when the nocturnal hour had already sounded, Don Angelo descended to the street and approached the dressmaker's door.

"You must understand that you can't go on like this . . ." He repeated his kind words, resuming the conversation. "Tell me the truth, tell me you've decided to come to Palermo after we take your poor sister to the hospice . . ."

"I wish I could tell you that I'd already been there for a while! What am I doing here? But . . . understand me . . . so many months without work . . . It isn't like the other time when at least I had put aside the money for the journey . . ."

"I've thought about that. If we're decided . . . But we'll plan better tomorrow. Buona notte, Mariangeli'!"

And he was about to leave. But he stayed a moment, without speaking, without moving, wavering. Then, since it was dark, he took her face in his hands, and removing the black kerchief, he kissed her forehead, delicately, as if she were his sister. His eyes filled with tears because he loved her and because he knew that he, only he, might bring her good fortune. . . . But he knew as well that this creature had already been marked for tragedy; she was a flower that someone would pick, sooner or later, but he didn't want to let her be picked before his eyes. . . .

These thoughts at once saddened and worried Angelo.

But Mariangelina had leaned her head on his shoulder, and she felt happy with that first kiss, so respectful and gentle, and again she was drunk, dazed, as when, hanging on Angelo's arm, trustfully, she walked forever through the great streets of Palermo.

(1918)

We're Talking Millions

Andrea Camilleri

"SIR? SIR? That you, sir, in person?"

What fucking time was it? He glanced at the alarm clock on the bedside table, thoroughly befogged by sleep. Five thirty in the morning. He figured if Catarella were waking him up at that hour, knowing the consequences he'd be facing, it meant the thing was pretty serious.

"What happened, Catarè?"

"They found Signora Pagnozzi's car, hers and her husband's, the Commendatore's."

The commendatore Aurelio Pagnozzi, one of the richest men in Vigàta, had disappeared with his wife the evening before.

"Only the car? Where were they?"

Born in Porto Empedocle in 1925, ANDREA CAMILLERI *lives in Rome. After working for many years in the theater as a director and playwright, he began to write fiction that draws on Italian dialects, especially Sicilian. His bestselling crime novels, set in the imaginary Sicilian town of Vigàta, feature the police inspector Salvo Montalbano. Three have been translated into English:* The Shape of Water *(1994),* The Terra-Cotta Dog *(1996), and* The Snack Thief *(1996).*

"Inside the car, sir."

"And what were they doing?"

"What could they be doing, sir, dead as doornails?"

"Why are they dead?"

"Sir, how could they be alive? The car fell into a gorge a hundred meters deep!"

"Catarè, you're telling me they were victims of a car accident? It wasn't provoked by some third party?"

There was a telling pause from Catarella, not so much pregnant as weightless.

"I don't know nothing about this third party, sir, 'cause Fazio visited the scene and didn't tell me they'd gone to parties."

"Catarè, who told you to call me?"

"No one, sir. I got this idea on my own. Besides, if I didn't tell you now about it, later you might get mad as hell."

"Catarè, do you realize we're not the highway patrol?"

"This is just what I wanted to ask you about, sir: if someone gets killed on some highway, who gets the case, us or the highway patrol?"

"I'll explain it to you later, Catarè."

Inspector Montalbano put down the phone, closed his eyes, wasted five minutes in an effort to nab the sleep that had escaped, cursed, then got up.

By seven he was at the office, in a mood black as ink.

"Where is Catarella? I'd like to have a word with him."

"He just went home," answered Galluzzo, who had relieved him at the switchboard. Fazio turned up.

"And so? What's the story with Pagnozzi and his wife?"

"Nothing, sir, they're both dead. Last night Pagnozzi's son Giacomino comes to see us, saying his father and mother didn't get back home by eight, as they'd planned. He waited a good hour, then called them on their cell. They didn't answer. He started to get worried, asked around here and there. Nobody knew anything. At ten thirty, more or less, he came to tell us the latest. I told him, seeing as how they were adults, we wouldn't search for them until twenty-four hours after the report was filed. He said something to me and left, furious."

"What did he say?"

"We could pound the report up our asses."

"You weren't the only one who spoke to him?"

"No, it was just me, but he blamed everybody, including the inspector."

"Fine. Go on."

"About four in the morning he phoned and Catarella called me. He'd found them. At the foot of a gorge. The signora, who was at the wheel, must've lost control or nodded off—they haven't figured it out yet. The car didn't catch fire, but it was totaled. While I was there, Officer Augello also arrived."

"Why is that? Who notified him?"

"Giacomino Pagnozzi phoned him. I take it Augello was a friend of the family."

May their souls rest in peace. That morning Montalbano went to confer with the police superintendent at Montelusa. He arrived almost two hours before the appointment and spent the time jawing with Jacomuzzi in Forensics.

He returned and found Mimì Augello with a long face, as if he had just come back from the cemetery on All Saints' Day.

"The poor bastards! What a shock to see them in such horrible shape. The signora Stefania looked as if she'd been flattened by a truck. She was almost unrecognizable."

Something in his assistant's tone of voice set off a spark in the inspector's head. He was almost certain of it; he'd known Mimì for too many years.

"You were friends with the husband?"

"Yeah, him too."

"What do you mean 'too'? Who were you more friends with?"

"Poor Stefania."

"Just out of curiosity—since when have you been carrying on with ladies of a certain age? It must've been a while since Pagnozzi saw sixty."

"Well, you know, Stefania was his second wife. Pagnozzi married her after he was widowed."

"How did he come to meet this Stefania?"

"She was his secretary."

"I see. How old was she?"

"Never asked her. At a rough guess, I'd say just under thirty."

"Mimì, put your hand on your heart and be honest: did you go to bed with her?"

"Well, you know, a young woman that lovely . . . I tried, but with no hope because she was clearly in love with Pagnozzi."

"Are you kidding me? Apart from the thirty-year difference, Pagnozzi looked like a corpse. He was so disgusting he would've scared a serial killer to death."

"I'm not talking about Pagnozzi senior, but the son."

Montalbano was dumbfounded.

"What the hell are you telling me?"

"The truth. Giacomino's the child from Pagnozzi's first marriage; he's in his thirties. Half of Vigàta knew he and Stefania were lovers. Why do you think he got worked up after seeing they didn't return? Not over his father—he didn't give a fuck about his father—but over his stepmother. Last night, in front of her corpse, he passed out."

"Her husband knew about the affair?"

"Cuckolds are the last to know."

"Does Giacomino live in his father's house?"

"No, on his own."

The conversation then shifted to a different topic.

The following morning Montalbano called in Mimì Augello, who had been absent from the office the previous afternoon.

"Come in, Mimì, and close the door. You know I overlook some things, but if you decide not to show up at the station, at least let me know."

"Salvo, everybody from Fazio to Catarella has the number of my cell phone! Give me a ring and I'll be here."

"Mimì, you don't understand shit. You must be here, not ready to come into the office when you're called, like some plumber."

"Alright, I'm sorry. Fact is, I went around with the consultant from the insurance company."

"Which insurance company, Mimì?"

"I don't know where my head is . . . Pagnozzi's."

"Why are you messing with that stuff? Is there something that doesn't seem square to you?"

"Yes," said Augello firmly.

"Then talk."

"As you know, the car, a BMW, didn't catch fire even though the tank was nearly full at the time of the accident. OK: in the glove compartment there was a receipt for a complete overhaul dated the same day as the accident. We went to see the mechanic, Parrinello, you know him, the guy who owns the garage near the power plant. He said Giacomino had brought him the car—"

"Doesn't he have a car?"

"He has one, but when he has to leave Vigàta, he borrows his father's. He had to go to Palermo, so he took it. When he returned, he said he heard a strange noise in the engine. Parrinello told us, however, that the car was basically in good shape, except for little things. He turned it over to Stefania around six. She was with her husband."

"Did he know where they were going?"

"Of course. Giacomino told him. They had an appointment with a builder at their country house, a few kilometers from Vigàta. He confirmed it, but he said he left after about an hour. From then till the moment they were found, we know nothing more about them. Still, we can suppose—"

"What does the insurance company say?"

"They don't understand the accident. The BMW must've proceeded straight instead of making the turn. It traveled for roughly a hundred meters and then dropped into the gorge. There's no trace of any braking. Since it rained till the day before yesterday, you can clearly see the wheels heading straight for the gorge."

"Maybe the signora had an attack."

"Are you joking? The woman was a gym fanatic. She even did a survival course in Nairobi last year."

"What does Doctor Pasquano say?"

"He did the autopsies. Pagnozzi, given his age, was fine. Stefania, Pasquano said, was a perfect machine. They hadn't eaten or drunk anything. They'd made love."

"What?!"

"That's what Pasquano says. Maybe they got horny when the builder left. They had a furnished home at their disposal. The cell phone was switched off. After, when it was already dark and they had a nap, they got back on the road. And what happened happened. This seems the most plausible explanation."

"Indeed," responded the inspector, lost in thought.

"There's something more," continued Augello. "Pasquano showed me a detail that might explain the dynamic of the accident. Poor Stefania's fingernails were broken. Obviously in an attempt to open the door. She may have had a mild attack, revived, seen what was happening, and tried to open the door, but it was too late."

"Crap!" said Montalbano.

"What do you mean?"

"A young woman, as you've described her, athletic, survival course and so on, has sharp reflexes. If she revives from a mild attack and sees the car heading for a gorge, she doesn't try to open the door, but simply slams on the brakes. And the brakes, from what you've told me, were working fine."

"Crap," said Mimì Augello in turn.

When it was time to eat, the inspector, instead of taking the road that leads to his place in Marinella and wolfing down some sardines ("tomorra I make you them stuffed sardines," his maid Adelina had written in a note she left him the day before), he headed for Montelusa, turning off at a certain point into the San Giovanni area where the accident had occurred. At the second turn he drove straight, just as the Pagnozzis' BMW had done, and braked on the edge of the gorge. There were many tire marks, as well as the tracks of a special tow truck that had recovered the wreck. Montalbano stood on the edge of the gorge for a good while, smoking and thinking. Then he decided that he had earned the stuffed sardines, climbed into his car, swung around, and headed toward Marinella. The dish turned out to be first-rate; after Montalbano had eaten, he felt as if he might start purring like a cat.

Instead he picked up the phone, called his friend Ingrid Sjostrom, Cardamone by marriage. She was a Swede who had been a car mechanic in her country.

"Hullo? Hullo? Who's dere?"

Casa Cardamone tended to have exotic maids. This one must have been an Australian aboriginal.

"It's Montalbano. Is Signora Ingrid there?"

"Yez."

He heard Ingrid's steps approaching the phone.

"Salvo! How lovely! It's been ages."

"Can we meet tonight?"

"Of course. I had an engagement, but it fell through. When do we meet?"

"At nine. The usual bar in Marinella."

Ingrid looked stunning, decked out for fall in jacket and trousers, very elegant. They had an apéritif. Montalbano heard distinctly, as if they had been spoken aloud, the curses of sudden impotence that the males in the place mentally hurled at him.

"Listen, Ingrid: do you have time?"

"All the time you want."

"Fine. Let's do something. Let's finish the drinks and go eat in a trattoria near Montereale where, I've heard, the cooking isn't bad. Then we'll head to my place. We have to wait till it gets dark."

Ingrid smiled impishly.

"Salvo, there's no need for the dark to be really dark. It's enough just to close the shutters and it'll seem like night-time, don't you think?"

Ingrid always aroused him and he always had to pretend nothing was happening. When he was a tyke and went to do "his duty," that is to say, the things owed to God, the catechism, the priest explained that sins, in order to qualify as sins, didn't need to be enacted; it was enough to think them. If things stood thus, the inspector, with regard to sins of commission with Ingrid, had scored an absolute zero; he could appear before the Lord pure as an angel. With regard to thoughts, things changed radically: he would have been thrown into the depths of hell. It wasn't Ingrid who stopped what normally happens between a man and a woman; it was that he—he couldn't betray Livia. And the Swede, with typical feminine guile, would-n't let him rest.

The trattoria was almost empty, so Montalbano could show Ingrid what he had in mind without playing the role of conspirator. At the inspector's house, Ingrid changed clothes. The trousers that Montalbano gave her reached the middle of her calves. They set off in the car again,

heading toward the San Giovanni area. There Ingrid did
what the inspector had asked her to do, and she succeeded
at the first try. They returned to Marinella. Ingrid
undressed, took a shower. She didn't want to be escorted
to the nearby bar where they had met and where she had
left her car. She left the house singing to herself. Holy
Madonna, what a woman! She hadn't even raised the issue
of why he'd subjected her to that risky experiment. Nothing. She just said, if a friend who was a friend asked her for
a favor, she did it and that was that. If Livia had been in
the Swede's place that night, his mouth would've been dry
as sand from all the answers and explanations.

He went to sleep as soon as his head hit the pillow. He
hardly had time to close his eyes.

Although the weather in the morning was a bit unsettled
and clouds occasionally hid the sun, Montalbano seemed
to be in a good mood to his men at the station.

"Send in Officer Augello and hold my calls."

Mimì arrived in a hurry.

"Sit down, Mimì, and listen to me. If Pagnozzi happened to die alone, through his own fuck-up, who would've
received the inheritance?"

"The wife. Plus some small change for the son. They
didn't get along so hot."

"Is it a huge inheritance?"

"We're talking millions."

"What if the wife died too? Who'd get it?"

"Giacomino, the son. Unless some conflicting will exists."

"Does it exist?"

"So far it hasn't come to light."

"I don't believe it will."

"Why are you asking me all these questions?"

"Because I've got an idea, which has been, in a certain sense, confirmed by the facts. I'll tell you what I think; you do the rest."

"Sure. Talk."

"Let's say, then, that Signora Stefania goes with her husband to pick up the car that Parrinello has overhauled. From there they go to the country house to talk to the builder. When he leaves, the signora gets all hot and bothered and they go to the bedroom. Pagnozzi must be happy; I wouldn't think they had much of a love life, seeing, as you've told me, she was in love with her stepson. And you know why she did it, Mimì?"

"Tell me."

"Because she needed it to be dark. They get dressed and head back to Vigàta. The road is deserted. Before the second turn, she puts her husband out of commission, a knock on the head with something; if she doesn't kill him, at least she stuns him. She proceeds slowly toward the gorge, there's no need to hurry, we're the ones who imagine the car moving at a fast clip. When the BMW is suspended in the air, she tries to open the door and throw herself out."

"But she would've died too!"

"No, Mimì, here's where you get it all wrong. True, there's a gorge, but it comes after a sort of terrace, five to six meters long and two meters deep. The signora figured she'd land there while the car with her husband dropped into the gorge. But the door didn't open, even though she broke her nails trying to get it open."

"What are you telling me?"

"It was this detail from the autopsy that made me suspicious. Why didn't she brake? Why did she only try to throw herself out?"

"Are you sure about what you're saying?"

"I tested it with Ingrid last night."

"You're crazy! You endangered that woman's life. You're both irresponsible!"

"Since when? Yesterday after lunch I went to buy four iron stakes and twenty meters of rope, and before the experiment Ingrid and I fenced off the outer boundary of the terrace. You want to know something? Ingrid landed well within the enclosure; Signora Stefania, with all her work at the gym and the survival school, could've easily managed it. And if she showed up later with bruises and abrasions, so much the better: the wounds would've reinforced her story. Namely, that she suffered an attack, realized too late what was happening, opened the door, and jumped. Then she would've burst into tears over the unfortunate death of her poor old husband. Only to go and enjoy the inheritance with the man of her dreams, her beloved Giacomino."

Mimì Augello remained speechless for a while; his brain was grinding away. Then he decided to speak.

"In your view, therefore, it's a question of premeditated murder, not a brief attack or a mechanical breakdown."

"Precisely."

"But if the car was in perfect condition, why didn't the door open?"

Montalbano didn't respond; he continued to look straight at his assistant. "He's getting the drift now," he thought, "because he too can think like a cop."

Mimì Augello started to reason out loud.

"Parrinello, the mechanic, couldn't have manipulated the door."

"Tell me why."

"Because they got out of the car when they reached the country house, right? If the door didn't work well, Stefania wouldn't have dreamed of endangering her life; she would've postponed everything till a better opportunity presented itself. Nor could the builder have done it."

"So, Mimì, you're telling me that another plan had been added to the plan. Someone who was privy to how Stefania was going to knock off her husband intervened to tamper with the door. Try a little harder, Mimì."

"Christ!" Augello suddenly exclaimed.

"Precisely, Mimì. The beloved Giacomino didn't stay at home awaiting the arrival of his father and his lover-stepmother. They'd cooked up the plan together, he and Stefania. When the woman, as if following a script, goes to bed to play hide the salami with her husband, Giacomino, who is holed up in the vicinity, comes out of his lair and fiddles with the door so that, once closed, it can't be opened again. You said we're talking millions. Why split it with a woman who at any moment might blackmail you? When Stefania climbs into the car to kill her husband, she doesn't know that by closing the door she has also closed her grave. And now, Mimì, get out of this one."

At the end of the third day of interrogation, Giacomino Pagnozzi confessed to the murder.

(1999)

Further Reading

Although the perennial problem with modern Italian literature in English is finding books in print, it remains possible to continue the geographical approach taken by the
this book and read more extended works set in Italian
locales. Northern Italy is intriguingly depicted in Gianni
Celati's stories of the Po valley, *Voices from the Plains* (1985),
in Giorgio Bassani's novel of the Ferrarese Jewish community under Fascism, *The Garden of the Finzi-Continis*
(1962), and in Italo Svevo's probing psychological portrait
of his Triestine narrator, *The Confessions of Zeno* (1923).
Paolo Barbaro's nonfiction work, *Venice Revealed* (1998),
offers an affectionate appreciation of the city. Enrico
Brizzi's novel about a love affair, *Jack Frusciante Has Left the
Band* (1995), energetically evokes youth subcultures in con-
temporary Bologna, which is also the setting of Carlo
Lucarelli's inventive mystery about a serial murderer,
Almost Blue (1997).

Rome is perhaps the Italian city best represented by
fiction in translation. Elsa Morante's novel, *History* (1974),
presents a richly detailed and moving treatment in the context of the Second World War. William Weaver's anthol-
ogy, *Open City: Seven Writers and Rome* (1999), gathers the

work of such major writers as Natalia Ginzburg and Alberto Moravia. Carlo Emilio Gadda's experimental murder mystery, *That Awful Mess on Via Merulana* (1957), and Pier Paolo Pasolini's novel of the impoverished suburbs, *A Violent Life* (1959), highlight the more infernal aspects of the city through remarkable casts of characters.

Southern Italy has inspired a broad range of narratives. The Fascist period provoked tales of resistance, such as Carlo Levi's memoir of his exile in Basilicata, *Christ Stopped at Eboli* (1945), and Ignazio Silone's novel about a peasant village in Abruzzo, *Fontamara* (1933). Post–World War II Naples can be glimpsed in Anna Maria Ortese's collection of stories, *The Bay Is Not Naples* (1953). The uneven economic development between the North and South figures in two quite different novels: Elio Vittorini's lyrical account of an emigrant's return home, *Conversation in Sicily* (1941), and Niccolò Ammaniti's suspenseful revelation of a kidnapping, *I'm Not Scared* (2001). Leonardo Sciascia's novels and stories, such as the collection *The Wine-Dark Sea* (1973), are suffused with the history and culture of his native Sicily, including the violent presence of the Mafia. Sicily has been the setting of historical novels that are at once affecting and revealing of Italian society, notably Giuseppe Tomasi di Lampedusa's *The Leopard* (1958) and Dacia Maraini's *The Silent Duchess* (1990).

Readers searching for additional works might consult Ray Keenoy and Fiorenza Conte's *Babel Guide to Italian Fiction in English Translation* (1995). This convenient guide not only lists titles, but provides short reviews.

Permissions

Every effort has been made to secure permission to translate and publish these stories. In those instances where we were unable to determine copyright holders, please contact Whereabouts Press.

Barbara Alberti, "Wicked Memories." Selections from Alberti, *Memorie malvage*, Venice: Marsilio, 1976, pp. 17–20, 39–46, 71–73, 122–123.

Corrado Alvaro, "Honeymoon in Naples." "Viaggio di nozze a Napoli," in Alvaro, *L'amata alla finestra*, Milano: Bompiani, 1994, pp. 67–71. Translated and published by permission of Bompiani, Milan.

Romano Bilenchi, "A Geographical Error." "Un errore geografico," in Bilenchi, *Anna e Bruno e altri racconti*, Milano: Rizzoli, 1997, pp. 53–60. Translated and published by permission of Agenzia Letteria Internazionale.

Massimo Bontempelli, "My Civil Death." "La mia morte civile," in Bontempelli, *La donna dei miei sogni e altre storie d'oggi*, Milano: Mondadori, 1925, pp. 42–49. Translated and published by permission of the author's heirs.

Dino Buzzati, "The Bewitched Jacket." "La giacca stregata," in Buzzati, *Il colombre e altri racconti*, Milano: Mondadori, 1966, pp. 173–181.

Andrea Camilleri, "We're Talking Millions." "Stiamo parlando di miliardi," in Camilleri, *Gli arancini di Montalbano*, Milano: Mondadori, 1999, pp. 171–181.

Natalia Ginzburg, "Summer." "Estate," in Ginzburg, *Cinque romanzi brevi e altri racconti*, Torino: Einaudi, 1964, pp. 409–412.

Claudio Magris, "Music Lessons." Reprinted by permission of the author.

Luigi Malerba, "The Game." "Il gioco dello scippo," in Malerba, *Dopo il pescecane*, Milano: Bompiani, 1979, pp. 47–51.

Dacia Maraini, "The Other Family." "L'altra famiglia," in Maraini, *Mio marito*, Milano: Bompiani, 1968, pp. 55–66. Translated and published by permission of Bompiani, Milan.

Marilia Mazzeo, "Deep Water." "Acqua Alta," in Mazzeo, *Acqua alta*, Roma–Napoli: Theoria, 1998, pp. 162–168.

Maria Messina, "The Shawl." "Lo scialle" (1918), in Messina, *Le briciole del destino*, Palermo: Sellerio, 1996, pp. 9–19.

Alberto Moravia, "The Thinker." "Il pensatore," in Moravia, *Racconti romani*, Milano: Bompiani, 1954, pp. 63–69. Translated and published by permission of Bompiani, Milan.

Aldo Palazzeschi, "The Lady with the Fan." "La signora dal ventaglio," in Palazzeschi, *Tutte le novelle*, Milano: Mondadori, 1957, pp. 644–654.

Goffredo Parise, "Well Off." "Benessere borghesia," in Parise, *Borghesia e altre voci escluse dai sillabari*, Pistoia: Via del Vento, 1997, pp. 3–10.

Luigi Pirandello, "The Black Kid." "Il capretto nero" (1913).

Domenico Rea, "The American Woman." "L'americana," in Rea, *Tentazione e altri racconti*, Napoli: Società Editrice Napoletana, 1976, pp. 135–149. Translated and published by permission of the author's heirs.

Lalla Romano, "The Air of Rome." "L'aria di Roma," in Romano, *La villeggiante*, Torino: Einaudi, 1975, pp. 35–41.

Alberto Savinio, "Noontide at Anacapri." "Meriggio ad Anacapri," in Savinio, *Capri*, Milano: Adelphi, 1988, pp. 53–69.

Tiziano Scarpa, "Built to Kill." "Le pietre assassine," in Scarpa, *Venezia é un pesce: una guida*, Milano: Feltrinelli, 2000, pp. 105–113.

Mario Rigoni Stern, "Enchantment." "Malia," in Rigoni Stern, *Sentieri sotto la neve*, Torino: Einaudi, 1999, pp. 45–51.

Antonio Tabucchi, "Voices Borne by Something, Impossible to Say What." "Voci portate da qualcosa, impossibile dire cosa," in Tabucchi, *L'angelo nero*, Milano: Giangiacomo Feltrinelli Editore SpA, 1991, pp. 11–27.

Federigo Tozzi, "A Bender." "Una sbornia" (1920).

About the Translator

LAWRENCE VENUTI (1953–) is a translator of Italian literature as well as a translation theorist and historian. He has translated works by Barbara Alberti, Dino Buzzati, Milo De Angelis, and I.U. Tarchetti. Recent translations include Juan Rodolfo Wilcock's *The Temple of Iconoclasts* and Antonia Pozzi's *Breath: Poems and Letters*. He has investigated the practice of translation in such books as *The Translator's Invisibility* (Routledge), and he reviews Italian fiction for the *New York Times*. He is currently professor of English at Temple University.